REMARKABLE
TREES
OF THE WORLD

IN MEMORY OF MY FATHER, WHO DIED
WHILE I WAS AWAY HUNTING TREES

TEXT AND PHOTOGRAPHS BY

THOMAS PAKENHAM

REMARKABLE
TREES
OF THE WORLD

W. W. NORTON & COMPANY
NEW YORK · LONDON

Contents

Introduction
Another Sixty

SIX YEARS AGO I WROTE *Meetings with Remarkable Trees*. My friends, who knew my books on African history, expressed mild surprise. At the time it appeared, even to my publishers, a fanciful idea for me to write a book about sixty individual trees, or groups of trees. But it seemed to strike a chord with the public. People wrote to tell me that they secretly hugged trees but had been too embarrassed to admit it. Others said they had never seen much point in trees, but now they looked at them with new eyes. A South African told me I was a hero in his family. 'You see, our mother's 95, half blind and she's lost her marbles. She thinks your book's absolutely wonderful.' I hope all this did not go to my head.

I chose the first sixty trees arbitrarily, perhaps even whimsically. There were only three principles. Each tree must be alive (or dead on its feet) in Britain or Ireland. It must have a strong personality, in fact so strong that my wife (not a fanatical admirer of trees herself) will cry 'Wow' when we walk together into its presence. And it must have a good face, meaning that it presents a face to my camera which will make a portrait.

I have now chosen another sixty trees on the same principles, with one difference. These trees, or groups of trees, are scattered across the world *beyond* Britain and Ireland. Recklessly, my publishers have let me make the world into my oyster. And who wouldn't jump at that chance? I have spent four wild years roaming the world, and ransacking it for trees with noble brows and strong personalities. Like the first volume, this new tree book won't help you identify trees, let alone grow them. But I hope it will help you meet some new ones, and you too will cry 'Wow' when you stand in their presence.

Sometimes one follows the trail of an ancient tree, like a hunter tracking a white rhino through the bush, and finds it already dead. Worse, the trees for which you are yourself responsible, the trees in your own garden, are maimed or shattered by storms. Ten years ago, at my family's home in Ireland we had a garden and park teeming with 200-year-old beeches. My favourite was a venerable creature with five trunks. It was the star of *Meetings with Remarkable Trees* – the snow-encrusted giant which featured on the frontispiece, end papers and in the body of the text. As I said then, it was on borrowed time. You can see it in the two photographs above: before and after the Boxing Day storm in the final year of the millennium. It still lies there today in the wind and the rain, its five trunks splayed open like five fingers, a monument rather than a corpse. I haven't

Top and above: END OF A FAMILY TREE – BEFORE AND AFTER THE STORM OF DECEMBER 26, 1999
Page 2, FRONTISPIECE: THE MONTEZUMA CYPRESS AT TULE, MEXICO – BIGGEST GIRTHED TREE IN THE WORLD
Page 4: 'THE SENATE' – A GROUP OF GIANT SEQUOIAS AT SEQUOIA NATIONAL PARK, CALIFORNIA

the heart to cut it up for firewood. I feel its loss like a sort of bereavement.

It was the loss of other great beeches in the early 1990s, old friends to our family in Ireland, that gave me the original idea for *Meetings*. I felt I had been taking the friendship of these trees for granted. The inspiration for this new book came from two rather different encounters.

The first was in America in August 1992, on the bewitching island called Martha's Vineyard. I was strolling down the main street of Edgartown when I was astonished to see a huge Pagoda tree, *Sophora japonica,* leap out of the pavement ahead of me, like a dolphin from a tank. Good heavens, I said to myself. This must be *the* champion Pagoda tree, the biggest in the world outside China or Japan – and knowledgeable friends told me I was right. But when I came to look it up in the Register of American Champion Trees, a sort of social register of tree society, I found no sign of this Chinese giant to which someone – apparently a sea captain, Thomas Milton – had given the freedom of the pavement in Martha's Vineyard. The explanation was as astonishing as the tree. The tree was not in the register because it was neither native nor naturalised. It was an alien, a non-tree or un-tree. It didn't exist for the purpose of the register. Good heavens, I said again. America must be bursting with great trees, must have great trees beyond the dreams of plenty, if it can tell a giant Pagoda tree to go back to China. A decade later, I found I was right. Almost all the old-growth forests in Europe were felled centuries ago. Some survive in America, especially the west. For the wandering tree hunter, the American west is paradise regained.

The second encounter was in South Africa in November 1996. I had been on the stump promoting *Meetings* in the vibrant world of shopping malls. What about a quiet weekend with elephants and baobabs, said my kindly publisher. We took our malaria pills and drove 300 miles to Kruger National Park. I knew a little about elephants, but the baobabs, which so resemble them – and outshine them – were a revelation. Outside the park, at Klaserie, we met one huge, hollow creature which had been used as a bar during the gold rush of the 1880s. In those days the bar was wide enough, we were told, to serve 15 miners abreast inside the tree. Now the door had nearly closed itself with new growth and there were only empty bottles inside. But this encounter was the start of a dangerous love affair with baobabs. It has needed the self-control of a monk not to let them take over this book.

Above: PAGODA TREE IN THE STREET AT EDGARTOWN, MARTHA'S VINEYARD, MASSACHUSETTS – BELIEVED TO HAVE BEEN PLANTED ABOUT 1833 BY A SEA CAPTAIN, THOMAS MILTON, WHO HAD BROUGHT IT FROM THE ORIENT IN A POT

Like the first volume, this book owes little to conventional botany. It is arranged according to the personality of the trees: Giants, Dwarfs, Methusalehs, Dreams, Trees in Peril. In contrast to the first volume, where most of the sixty trees were exotic invaders from abroad, most of these trees are natives. Some are the world champions of the species, trees of colossal age and size, whose young descendants I knew in Britain and Ireland.

In Giants, I include General Sherman, a giant sequoia in California, at 1500 tons the largest tree in the world – indeed the largest single living thing in the world. (I exclude the giant fungus, the size of a football pitch, hidden in northern Michigan. No one has ever seen it, as it lives underground, and it's not a *thing* but a collection of fungi sharing the same clone.) In Methusalehs, I include the wind-blasted bristlecone pines of the White Mountains of California. One of them, Old Methuselah himself, was found to be 4600 years old, making him the oldest tree yet measured by scientists. Shrines include some of the holiest trees in the world, like the immense camphor trees preserved in Shinto shrines in Japan and the 2200-year-old Bo tree in Sri Lanka, a cutting from the actual tree under which Buddha found enlightenment. Trees in Peril are the trees under attack by predatory loggers and impoverished farmers. It includes the exotic baobabs of Madagascar, now threatened by intensive farming, and the great spruce and Douglas fir and red cedars of Pacific America and Canada, in whose defence the conservationists have been fighting the loggers for decades.

In fours years of travelling, I came to owe countless debts of gratitude to people who gave help and support. The following list names some of those who helped me most:

IN AUSTRALIA: Rachel Blythe, Ross Ingram, Kingsley Dixon, Peter Valder, Peter and Nancy Underhill, Rose Talbot, Neil Parker, Tim McManus, David Richmond, Francis and Julie Keegan, John Morton, Georgina Persse, Sally and Roo Wright. IN NEW ZEALAND: Lynnaire Ryan, Carola and Michael Hudson, Stephen King. IN CANADA: Sally and Keith Sacré, Joe and Joanne Ronsley, Kim McArthur and Sherie Hodds, Michael Reynolds, Gordon Weetman and John Worrall, Jillian Stewart. IN TURKEY: Tricia and Timothy Daunt, Jane Baz and Vali Hüsnu Akdesir in Antalya. IN JAPAN: Mrs Hatakeyama, Mr Hiroshi Hayakawa, Masanori Owa, Hideo Suzuki, Mr Hiroaki Matsuyama, Sir Stephen Gomershall, Yuriko Akishima, Tom Kiley, Dennis Kiley. IN PORTUGAL: Louis

Above: A BAOBAB FOR THIRSTY MINERS DURING THE GOLDRUSH AT KLASERIE, SOUTH AFRICA

Vambeck. IN ITALY: Lupo Osti, Brother Michele of San Francesco, Verrucchio. IN BELGIUM AND HOLLAND: Philippe de Spoelberch, Ghislaine de Spoelberch, Alain Camu, Jeroen Pater. IN GERMANY: Heribert Reif, Gisela Doenig. IN FRANCE: Professor Robert Bourdu, Sybille and André Zavriew, Georgina Howell and Christopher Bailey. IN MEXICO: My nephew Damien Fraser and Paloma Fraser, Adrian Thorpe. IN THE U.S.A.: Bob and Kathy Van Pelt, Chip Mueller and Angela Ginorio, Evgenia and Julian Sands, Ron Lance, Guy Sternberg, John Palmer, Edith Spink, Diana Rowan Rockefeller, Bob Pirie. IN SOUTH AFRICA: Jim and Barbara Bailey, Prospero and Anna Bailey, Jessica and John Clarke, Beesie and Nicky Bailey, Jonathan Ball and Pam Bowling, Jonathan Bowling, Therese Herbert. IN IRELAND AND BRITAIN: Olda and Desmond FitzGerald, Mary McDougall, Grey and Neiti Gowrie, Mark Girouard, Patrick and Anthea Forde, Jane Martineau and Willy Mostyn-Owen, Christopher and Jenny Bland, Lindy Dufferin, Moira Woods, Michael and Dina Murphy, James and Alyson Spooner, Jacky and Julian Thompson, Kate and Patrick Kavanagh, Nella and Stan Opperman, Pilly Cowell, Liam and Maureen O'Flanagan, Paddy and Nicky Bowe, David and Linda Davies, Aaron Davis, Fionn Morgan, Daria and Alexander Schouvaloff, Simone Warner, Maurice and Rosemary Foster, Alison and Brendan Rosse, Aubrey Fennell, David Alderman.

I must single out for special thanks two distinguished botanists who guided my footsteps and my pen: Charles Nelson and Stephen Spongberg. Once again I must record how much I owe Angelo Hornak for recommending the mighty Linhof camera (though he warned me I would never be able to use it). I must thank the staff of Weidenfeld in London for working so hard in all stages of growing this book – from the seedling to the sturdy plant – especially Anthony Cheetham, Michael Dover and David Rowley. I must thank Mike Shaw, Jonathan Pegg and the staff of Curtis Brown. And to my overseas publishers – Bob Weil of Norton's in New York, and Jonathan Ball in Johannesburg – I owe a similar debt. Finally, I must thank my far-flung family – now a tribe of 59 brothers, sisters, children, grandchildren, nephews, nieces, great-nephews and great-nieces. Many helped with this book, but I can mention only three: my mother, my sister Antonia and my wife Valerie. All three have connived, often against their better judgement, to promote my reckless love affair with trees.

Above: GOATS PAYING THEIR RESPECTS TO ARGAN THORNS NEAR AGADIR, MOROCCO

GODS

I tell of Giants from times forgotten
Those who fed me in former days:
Nine worlds I can reckon, nine roots of the Tree,
The wonderful Ash, way under the ground.

THE CREATION OF THE WORLD FROM VOLUSPÀ (TR. P.B. TAYLOR)

Last of the Maori Gods

THE SUBTROPICAL RAIN BEGAN AGAIN as I tramped along the boardwalk to photograph Te Matua Ngahere (Father of the Forest) and Tane Mahuta (Lord of the Forest). These are the names that the Maori gave these two giant kauri trees before Captain Cook and the first Englishmen bravely set foot in New Zealand.

Kauris were by far the largest living things in the Maori world and they revered them like gods. Nineteenth-century English settlers found they made divine timber. Today, these two trees are part of less than a dozen giant kauris (*Agathis australis*) that have survived 200 years of logging in New Zealand. Both have been given sanctuary at Waipoua State Forest, 250 miles north of Auckland. But we shall never know much about the other Maori tree-gods. The loggers disposed of the largest and tallest kauris more than a century ago.

I peered through the rain at the first kauri, Te Matua Ngahere. Yes, you could call it god-like. It was not merely the heroic dimensions of the smooth, grey, reticulated trunk: 60 feet in girth at a man's breast height and hardly tapering an inch for the next 50 feet. Above the trunk rose half a dozen huge grey branches splayed out like fingers and supporting a jungle kingdom of their own. I saw orchids and clubmoss and a sinister strangler, the rata, which had sprung to life high in a fork and then dropped to the ground a long, predatory root like a drainpipe. (This strangler, you would think, had bitten off more than it could chew. But a hundred-year wait is nothing to a hungry strangler.)

The rain stopped and, on the slippery boardwalk, I clamped my ponderous Linhof camera to its tripod. A notice warned tourists not to leave the boardwalk. But I needed a pygmy by the tree to show its scale. Should I – *dare* I be that pygmy? Boardwalks are designed to protect trees' delicate roots from the hammering of countless human feet. They also make good photographs impossible. There was one alternative to breaking the rules. Friends had told me about a friendly ecologist, Stephen King, who made regular visits to the jungle kingdom above the kauri's trunk, descending Tarzan-like on a rope from a nearby tree. What a picture it would make! I could see Tarzan's rope dangling from a branch. But that day there was no sign of Tarzan.

There are times when a man must do what a man must do. I explained to a dare-devil English tourist how to fire my camera shutter. Then, risking my life and good name, I wrapped myself in my scarlet photographic blanket and plunged through the undergrowth towards the trunk of the great tree. The photograph came out well I believe (judge for yourself) although I looked a bit odd, after burrowing like a rat under a razor-wire fence hidden in the ferns.

Next day the sun shone and I set off to see the second and even bigger kauri,

Preceding page: 'TE MATUA NGAHERE' (FATHER OF THE FOREST) AT WAIPOUA, NEW ZEALAND – THE BIGGEST GIRTHED KAURI

Pages 10–11: THE DOUBLE BAOBAB AT KHUBU ISLAND, BOTSWANA. WE LANDED ON THE SALTPAN

Opposite: 'TANE MAHUTA' (LORD OF THE FOREST) AT WAIPOUA, NEW ZEALAND – BIGGEST IN VOLUME OF ALL THE SURVIVING KAURIS. BUT THE LOGGERS TOOK EVEN BIGGER ONES

Opposite: GENERAL VIEW
OF TANE MAHUTA

Tane Mahuta. Of course I would get permission to leave the boardwalk. Why hadn't I thought of this earlier? But the ranger to whom I applied was preoccupied. He said he had just received a report that a tourist had arrogantly crossed the barrier protecting Te Matua Ngahere the previous afternoon. 'And there he stood,' said the outraged ranger, 'smirking into the camera, *smirking,* his face gashed by the wire, his back covered in mud.' I felt this was not the moment to ask for permission to see Tane Mahuta, and quietly slipped away, keeping my muddy back and battle-scars well-concealed. My self-restraint was rewarded. The same afternoon I heard that Stephen King, the ecologist, was working by Tane Mahuta, and would pose for my camera by the trunk.

Tane Mahuta is smaller-girthed than Te Matua Ngahere but bigger in every other respect: taller, at 150 feet from head to toe, and with outstretched branches to match. Eighty feet up in the canopy there is another jungle kingdom of mosses, ferns and stranglers – and another haunt of Stephen King. I wished I had had the courage to follow him on his rope. Anyway, he was earthbound that afternoon, repairing the damage to the roots inflicted by heavy rain. He worked barefoot, dressed in brown, looking more like a wood-elf than Tarzan, I discovered. When the photograph of Tane Mahuta was developed (see opposite) the wood-elf was barely visible by the trunk.

The Hyena and the Baobabs

LONG BEFORE AFRICA WAS OPENED UP by European explorers, the news of the baobab had astonished the world of science. Michel Adanson, a French naturalist, stumbled on the tree in the Cape Verde Islands, off the coast of West Africa. He noted the tree's stupendous size (twice the girth of any tree in Europe), its bizarre appearance (more like a pumpkin than a tree), and its extraordinarily soft, pith-like wood, which an elephant can tear off and chew when it feels thirsty. The great Carolus Linnaeus, Swedish count and guru of all 18th-century naturalists, paid Adanson the compliment of naming the genus after him. But the African baobab, *Adansonia digitata*, has continued to baffle scientists till the present day.

You can find elephantine baobabs in 20 African countries south of the Sahara. There are probably thousands of giant baobabs alive today, looming out of the parched thorn-scrub of savannah and low veld. Yet no one knows, within 1000 years, how old are the more ancient specimens. This is because the old trees are hollow, like most old trees; worse, most botanists have found that the surviving tree rings on the narrow rind of bark are impossible to count because they are so faint. Then consider the mysterious sex life of baobabs. Are they impregnated by bats or by some other creatures? And what other tree could have attracted the reputation of suddenly disappearing, as the baobab apparently can, when it succumbs to spontaneous combustion?

Nothing seems certain about the tree except that mythology comes to it naturally. It is the tree that, among many African peoples, is believed to be the home of their ancestral spirits. (Hence the need in Zambia in the 1960s to evacuate these spirits when their personal baobabs were about to be flooded by the Kariba dam. The evacuation was done by breaking off branches from the doomed trees and attaching them to new trees outside the danger zone.) And it is, in the creation myth, the 'Upside-down Tree'. When the Great Spirit made the world he gave each animal his own particular tree. The hyena got the baobab and threw it down in disgust, and the tree landed the wrong way up, with the roots sticking up like branches.

In 1998, I was offered the chance of going to see whether I agreed with the hyena. We set off, two in a small plane, two in a land cruiser, to visit some of the largest and finest baobabs in Botswana – especially a tree

Left: BAOBABS AT KHUBU ISLAND, BOTSWANA

Opposite: GREEN'S BAOBAB, BOTSWANA

Below: DETAILS OF GRAFFITI, INCLUDING 'GREEN'S EXPEDITION 1858'. LIVINGSTONE DIDN'T SIGN.

where Dr Livingstone, the great missionary-explorer, was supposed to have inscribed his initials.

The first was 'Green's Tree', called after the explorer whose expedition passed that way in 1858. We found it easily as Green had hacked 'Green's Expedition 1858' into the smooth pink bark on the lower side of the tree. I suppose if you are risking your life exploring the edge of the Kalahari Desert, you are allowed a little swagger, which could include being allowed to write your name on passing trees. But it sets a bad example. In fact Green *had* set a bad example. The world and his wife had followed and they had added their signatures – all except Livingstone. I liked Livingstone for that. He is rather a hero of mine – he behaved better to Africans than most of his fellow Europeans – and I was glad to find he had behaved better to trees.

The second was 'Chapman's Tree', called after another pioneer of Kalahari travel. There were no signatures on this tree. It was gigantic and stunningly beautiful, a perfect home for ancestral spirits. I photographed a young African

standing at its centre as if in homage. The great oval of curved trunks reminded me of a bronze sculpture by Rodin, formed by two curved hands, and entitled 'The Cathedral'.

But the climax of our trip was to come. About 100 miles to the south was Khubu Island, where the baobabs were said to be so wonderful that even the hyenas were delighted to live there.

It must be a poetic experience to sail in a boat to Khubu Island and spot the baobabs frisking like whales on the horizon. But the dry season lasts 10 months a year out here on the edge of the Kalahari Desert, and for most of that time the salt lake, the largest in Botswana, lives only as a series of mirages.

We crunched over the shimmering salt-pan in a land cruiser, following the fresh wheel tracks of someone who was heading for the island. (It would be foolish to get stuck 10 miles out from the shore.) Above our heads, two companions overtook us in the plane, which was the size of a large silver toy, its shadow stencilling, for a moment, the baobabs on the skyline, before being reunited with the plane as it landed.

Dr Livingstone was captivated by the baobabs of southern Africa. He compared them to giant radishes, carrots, parsnips. That makes good sense on the mainland. But here on Khubu Island the baobabs look more animal than vegetable, and marine animal at that: whales or hippos (appropriately, as *khubu* means 'hippo' in Tswana) or sea monsters. Whatever you call them, they are miraculous creatures. There is virtually no soil where they have made a home on Khubu Island. They have grown fat – fat beyond a pauper's dream – on smooth pink granite.

We pitched our tents under a grove of friendly-looking trees. Pay no attention to the local hyena, said my friends. 'Just keep your legs inside your tent when you're asleep and he won't dream of touching you.' I kept my legs inside my tent but I can't say I got much sleep. Twice I was woken by a hyena's laugh, which I didn't find particularly amusing.

At sunset the smooth skin of the baobabs seemed to glow with health, turning from pink to vermilion, like the granite rocks below them. Next day the overhead sun struck the rocks and trees with the force of a hammer on anvil. Although it was early autumn, the season for fruit, no seed-pods were hanging from the branches. The bright green leaves, shaped like a human hand (hence the species' name, *digitata*) were beginning to wither and fall. The 1990s saw a long run of unusually severe droughts in southern Africa – apparently the result of global warming. Even the Khubu baobab, the miraculous creature that springs from the rocks, has a limit to what it can bear.

As the plane's shadow sped across the shimmering salt-pan below us (it was my turn now to fly in the silver toy), a sombre thought took hold of me. In the next 20 years, when the world has become still warmer than it is now, will the baobabs desert Khubu and leave it to the hyenas?

Above: CHAPMAN'S BAOBAB, BOTSWANA

Opposite: DETAIL OF THE FIVE TRUNKS FORMING 'THE CATHEDRAL'

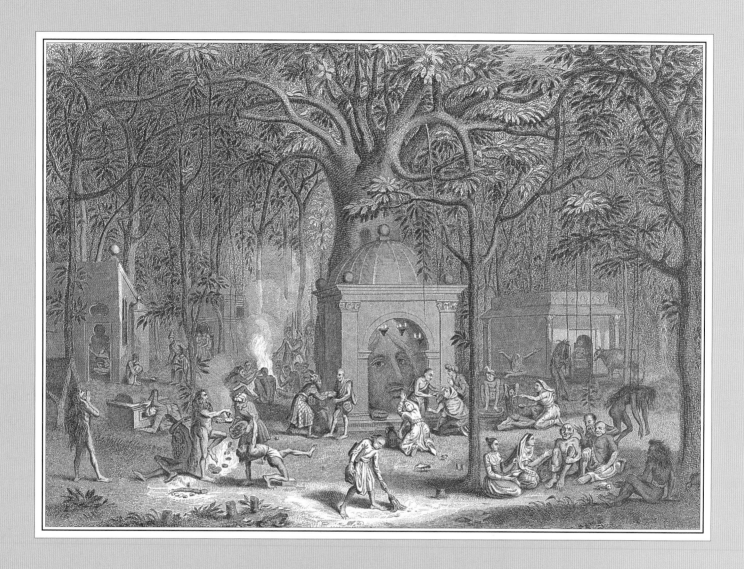

GODDESSES

Enter these enchanted woods
You who dare.
Nothing harms beneath the leaves...
Fair you fare.
Only at dread of dark
Quaver, and they quit their form;
A thousand eye-balls under hoods
Have you by the hair.
Enter these enchanted woods
You who dare.

GEORGE MEREDITH, THE WOODS OF WESTERMAIN

Saving the Great Mother Goddess

EIGHT YEARS AGO, IN 1994, THERE WAS PANIC in the small town of Tule, near Oaxaca city in the highlands of southern Mexico. Their own celebrated Tule cypress – El Arbol (The Tree), the tree where they sat at dusk and talked of the day's news, the tree that experts said was not only the biggest in Mexico, and the symbol of its power and pride before the Spanish conquest in the 16th century, but the biggest-girthed tree of any species ever recorded anywhere in the world – appeared to be dying.

Tree doctors were brought from as far afield as the Royal Botanic Gardens at Kew, near London. They looked at the 140-foot high specimen of Montezuma cypress (*Taxodium mucronatum*), with its astounding 190-foot girth, and they shook their heads. Once these immense vaulted branches, cusped and crocketed like the ribs of a Gothic cathedral, had swept down in bright green arcs to the ground. Now the leaves were turning yellow in spring and there were dead branches everywhere.

The tree was desperate for lack of water. That was what the Kew experts reported. *Tule* means 'marsh' in the local Zapotec dialect, and for centuries before the Spanish came the cypress had wallowed in a swamp of reed-mace fed by two local rivers. Then the swamp was drained, a church of Our Lady built facing the great tree (perhaps on the site of a Zapotec temple), gardens planted, and up grew a bustling colonial town where Indians came to sell straw hats and brightly coloured dresses and (perhaps in secret) figurines of the old gods.

Divert the traffic, fence off the tourists, water the tree. The doctors' blunt advice was followed. The patient began to recover. When I visited El Arbol in December 2001, the dead branches had been carefully cut away, and some of the wounds, painted white, were beginning to heal. The tree, weakened and mutilated, still radiates power. In fact the family to which it belongs, Taxodiaceae, could be called the most powerful of all botanical families. The Californian cousins of the Montezuma cypress, the coast redwood (*Sequoia sempervirens*) and giant sequoia (*Sequoiadendron giganteum*), are respectively the tallest and heaviest trees in the world. But the Montezuma cypress at Tule comes from a more numinous world. In California you can hug a giant sequoia, the soft, pink, spongy tube of bark tapering up in the mist above you. Here at Tule it is El Arbol that hugs *you*. It wraps itself around you, with its huge, bare brown arms, and its mane of bright green hair, a mother-goddess from the days of the Zapotecs, that could, if it stirred, squash us like so many woodlice.

Like its future, its past excites passion, and sometimes provokes its admirers to frenzy. Two questions dominate. Is it as ancient as it appears? And is it one tree or three?

First, its much contested age: 2000, 3000 years old, say the poets, politicians and PR persons – and why not? You might imagine that the biggest-girthed tree in the world was also one of the oldest. Yet the bark does not have a wizened look about it. Given a wet and warm summer, this is a species that can grow extremely fast. There is a Zapotec legend about the age of the tree: Pechocha, servant to Ehecatl, storm-god of the Aztecs, planted it for the people of Tule 1400 years ago. And, strange to say, some scientists agree with the legend. In the early 1920s,

Preceding page: THE MONTEZUMA CYPRESS AT TULE, OAXACA PROVINCE, MEXICO (DETAIL OF SOUTH-EAST SIDE)

Opposite: VIEW OF THE TULE CYPRESS FROM SOUTH-EAST

a botanist called Casiano Conzatti spent a whole year studying the tree, and counting the rings on the trunks of cypresses felled nearby. He announced that the tree was between 1433 and 1600 years old. Hey presto! But of course a bigger 'true' diameter would have made the tree over 2000 years old.

Second (and still more likely to incur the wrath of its admirers), dare one ask if it's really three trees masquerading as one? The controversy goes back at least as far as Alexander von Humboldt, the great German naturalist. He visited Mexico in 1803, and later wrote in his *Political Essay on New Spain:*

> In the village of Santa Maria del Tule…there is an enormous *sabino* [cypress], the trunk of which is 36 metres [120 feet] in circumference. This old tree is even more corpulent…than the dragon tree of the Canary Isles and any of the baobabs (Adansonia) of Africa. But examined closely…that *sabino* which is such a surprise to travellers is not a single individual but a group of three trunks united.

Today, the tree's admirers can reject Humboldt's insulting claim – or at least part of it. Recent DNA analysis proves that, genetically speaking, El Arbol is a single individual, not three separate seed-born trees that have grown together. But did three trunks, with identical genes, spring up from a single root? This certainly seems possible, although some scientists disagree. It would go some way to explain El Arbol's astounding girth. It would also – by some experts' reckoning – disqualify it from claiming the prize as the world's biggest-girthed tree.

Who cares, I asked myself, as I stood beneath its enormous arms last December, intoxicated by its beauty. Who cares? After all, it's the privilege of a god to have three natures, to be three-in-one and one-in-three.

Any Fool Can Climb a Gum Tree

ABOUT 250 MILES SOUTH OF PERTH, in the wettest and greenest corner of Western Australia, there were once some of the finest forests in the world: hundreds of thousands of acres of towering gum trees known by the Aboriginal name of *karri*. Most of the forests were turned into farmland and the great trees into rafters or beams or planks to build the city of Perth. But at least some of the oldest and biggest trees have been given shelter in national parks. Botanists call them *Eucalyptus diversicolor*, referring to the contrast in leaf colour. But it is the delicate marbling of the trunk, and its billowing foliage, as well as its enormous size (they can grow up to 300 feet high) that makes the karri, in my eyes, the noblest of all the 600 species of eucalyptus.

Three years ago, in 1998, I visited four of the tallest and most elegant, called 'The Four Aces'. The Four Graces would make a better name. They live in a clearing beside a small river and near a vineyard: an Arcadian spot. The sun was low by the time I had found them, and its dying light had splashed violet shadows on their marbled trunks and upper branches. I snatched a photograph, and a passer-by told me of three other gigantic karris nearby. 'You can climb *them.*' I thought he must be joking. Then I heard from a friend that these three karris were, until recently, used as lookouts for spotting forest fires. They were now one of Western Australia's tourist attractions. 'Why don't you have a go? Any fool can climb a gum tree. You're allowed to climb them – old ladies included. If you make it, they give you a printed testimonial.' How could I resist the challenge? Well, I did somehow. Then, in November 2001, I found myself on the north face of the Everest of the tree world.

The tallest lookout is the 207-feet-high Gloucester Tree (nothing much for a karri). Its spiral staircase – a ladder of steel spikes hammered into the living trunk – vanished into the forest canopy far above my head. I climbed slowly and, I trust, majestically upwards. The view from the lookout platform on top was obscured by low cloud. I had no temptation to linger. Far below, a line of determined old ladies had alighted from a tour bus and were marching towards the tree. The worst moment of the descent was when I felt something soft under my boot. It turned out to be somebody's hand. An old lady's? I didn't dare look down. Somehow we both survived the meeting.

When I reached the ground the ranger explained that they had stopped giving testimonials as it was such an easy climb. 'But surely you have failures too,' I said desperately. 'Three deaths since I came here,' said the ranger. 'All men. One dead on top, one fell and one died in the bus. All heart attacks. Could have happened anywhere.'

And to anyone. It was a miracle that I had got out alive.

Opposite: THE FOUR ACES, WESTERN AUSTRALIA, AT SUNSET. SHOULD THEY BE CALLED THE FOUR GRACES?

Below: THE GLOUCESTER TREE, WESTERN AUSTRALIA. I BEGIN THE 207-FOOT CLIMB UP THE SPIRAL OF STEEL SPIKES

Redwoods with Heads in the Clouds

CHARLES SARGENT, THE EBULLIENT DIRECTOR of the Arnold Arboretum at Boston, once said that the coast redwood of California was the most magnificent of all conifers, and the forests of coast redwood the most impressive evergreen forests in America. I think Sargent was right – about the forest, if not the tree.

Before the settlers came, there were two million acres of virgin redwood forest (*Sequoia sempervirens*) running for 500 miles along the fog-wrapped coast north from Monterey to the border with Oregon. The lumber was irresistible: cheap, cheerful and apparently everlasting. San Francisco was built with it. Today little more than 3 per cent of the original forests have been given permanent sanctuary in state parks and one national park. To save these remnants from the loggers has proved one of the Homeric struggles of conservation – a war of giants lasting more than a century –started by John Muir, taken up by the Save-the-Redwoods League, and continued even today by heroic activists (like 'Butterfly Hill', the girl who lived two years 200 feet up a redwood).

The remnants are still magical. But how do you photograph anything but the giants' feet? Their heads are often lost in the clouds, or in the dense fog-banks that roll in from the Pacific. Even under brilliant blue skies their heads, hidden in the dense canopy of the forest, are invisible to a person on the ground. But the experts have climbed them with ropes and measured them with lasers, and they can tell us, to one decimal point, which of these is the World's Tallest Tree.

The current champion is a 368.6 foot high redwood, 'Stratosphere Giant', also described, in rather a mouthful, as 'the world's tallest known living thing'. Its discoverer in the 1990s was a young scientist called Steve Silett specialising in the rarified air of redwood tree canopies. He and his rival big-tree hunters have found 26 redwoods over 360 foot high, 18 of which are in one part of Humboldt State Park. Competition for the title is intense and the identity of the winner changes almost daily. There are 86 redwoods known to have crossed the 350- foot mark, and many are growing faster than beanstalks. But whichever tree is the current champion it's certain to be a coast redwood. For years it's been known that the runners-up – the Australian mountain ash and the Douglas fir – are trailing far behind. Shorter still, though far bigger in volume and weight, is the other kind of Californian redwood, the giant sequoia that comes from the Sierras 200 miles to the east.

I drove through Humboldt State Park on a dreary day in November – and my blood raced. Somewhere far above me, head and shoulders taller than a 30-storey skyscraper, invisible in the rain and fog, was old Stratosphere, the Champ himself, all 368.6 feet of him. Individually

Opposite: COAST REDWOODS IN JEDEDIAH SMITH STATE PARK, CALIFORNIA

the trees are not so impressive – despite Sargent's claim – as the giant sequoias in the Sierras. But as an evergreen forest, vast and uniform, they exude a powerful current of magic – the brown trunks mesmeric, like marching feet, for twenty miles across the marshy flats of wood sorrel and sword fern.

A forest of goddesses? Not, I think, down here at Humboldt State Park. Further north, up the coast towards the Oregon border, the forests are still more magical – more exuberant (it rains even more) and set in a more poetic landscape, of spongy hills and deep ravines

The photographs here give hardly more than a taste. The first shows a glimpse of the forest outside the old logging town of Crescent City – a few thousand acres miraculously preserved as Jedediah Smith State Park. Even here, summer drought and forest fires jointly take their tax. But the Coast redwood, unlike its cousin in the Sierras and most other conifers, can regenerate from the stump, so the forest is full of young trees re-born from the blackened stumps of their parents.

The second photograph shows one of the more wayward of the Coast redwoods, the Corkscrew Tree at Prairie Creek State Park. I don't know many other goddesses twisted like barley-sugar. But I found the arrangement poetic: garlands of young redwood leaves from the ancient twisted trunk, while two younger trees, a hemlock and a mossy yellow big-leaved maple, bow low in homage.

Above: DETAIL OF A COAST REDWOOD IN JEDEDIAH SMITH STATE PARK, CALIFORNIA

Opposite: THE CORKSCREW TREE, A COAST REDWOOD AT PRAIRIE CREEK STATE PARK, CALIFORNIA

Nectar at the House of Representatives

Opposite: THE 'HOUSE OF REPRESENTATIVES' – GIANT SEQUOIAS IN SEQUOIA NATIONAL PARK, CALIFORNIA

STRANGE, YOU MIGHT SAY, TO INCLUDE A PACK of time-serving politicians in a section of this book devoted to goddesses. But the fault is not mine. These giant sequoias are elegant and feminine: cinammon-coloured titanesses, 40 or 50 feet round the waist, draped about the arms with swags of shining green, soaring 200 feet to the heavens. It was the vanity of male politicians, a century ago, to give them this incongruous name, 'The House', meaning the House of Representatives.

You can see how it happened. After 30 years of battering at the gates of power in Washington, the conservationists, inspired by a Scottish immigrant called John Muir, rescued most of the finest groves of giant sequoias (*Sequoiadendron giganteum*) from the axes and saws of the logging companies. The forest where this particular grove lies was saved for the nation in 1890 under the name of Sequoia National Park. Teddy Roosevelt, the bear-hunting President, was delighted to help. And the politicians, to reward themselves for their generosity with tax-payers' money, gave political names to many of the finest trees: 'Lincoln' (two separate trees), 'The President', 'The Senate', 'The House' and so on.

I had the good fortune to find myself tramping through this forest in deep snow at eight o'clock one morning in March. These huge trees are happy in the champagne air you breathe 6000 feet up in the Sierra Nevada (Snowy Mountains) on the Pacific side of the Rockies in California. In spring there's a kaleidoscope of rain and sun. In winter the tree roots are buttressed with snow. This seems like paradise.

Yet the seasons bring their ration of forest fires. You cannot avoid seeing their mark on most of the larger trees: a fire-wound burnt deep into the heartwood, despite the flameproof tannin in their veins and the asbestos-like wrapping of their bark. Sometimes an old tree on a steep slope, a tree that has accumulated fallen branches on the upper side of its trunk, is burnt out to a shell, and the park rangers don't intervene. They have learnt their lesson. Better a small wildfire started by lightning – or a small controlled fire to clean out the scrub round the great trunks – than a holocaust later. Fire is also essential if the giant sequoias are to breed (though a successor may only be necessary once every thousand years). Fire burns out the rival saplings of pine and fir, which have thinner bark and inflammable resin, not tannin, in their veins. Then it prepares a seed-bed of ashes into which the seeds of the giant sequoia are projected from the heated cones far above.

But these small fires occur only in summer when the park is full of rangers and trippers. In March, when it's empty and sun shines through the mist, you can stand at the snow-covered feet of these titanesses and feel like a god yourself – a god who has had one too many glasses of nectar.

The Bachelor and the Three Graces

Left: THE BACHELOR AND
THE THREE GRACES,
YOSEMITE NATIONAL
PARK, CALIFORNIA

JUST INSIDE THE SOUTHERN GATES of Yosemite National Park in California is one of the finest groves of giant sequoia, and it's called Mariposa Grove, after the Spanish word for 'butterfly'. An odd name, you might think, for a grove of 500-ton giants. But early in the 19th century Spanish and Mexican explorers gave this name to a settlement in the romantic pinewoods on the lower slopes of the Sierras. At this time the giant sequoias were still hidden in their mountain fastness above, known only to the local Indians; the first grove (at Calaveras, 50 miles north of Mariposa) were not discovered by Europeans until 1852, a decade after the United States had grabbed California from the Mexicans. Anyway the name is not inappropriate. Many of the trees at Mariposa are unusually elegant, especially the foursome known as the Bachelor and the Three Graces.

I took this photograph in mid-November, after the first winter storm had come and gone, leaving patches of slush among the shredded bark and empty cones at the feet of the trees. The sun was cool here at 6000 feet, the forest silent and almost deserted. In summer Yosemite boils over with visitors. Understandably, half the world seems to make an annual trip to see the wonders – the mighty canyons, the mile-high waterfalls – and Mariposa gets its share of awe-struck visitors. There is nothing new in this adulation. One of the first white men to admire Yosemite was President Lincoln who paused here in 1864 during the Civil War and declared Mariposa Grove and Yosemite valley a 'protected state reserve'. By the 1880s Mariposa could already boast of the 'most famous tree in the world' – the Wawona Tunnel Tree – which had been excavated to allow stage coaches to drive through its 'stomach'. Today this form of homage to giant trees has passed out of fashion. But in the 1880s it was considered good publicity for the campaign to save the coast redwoods and giant sequoias from the loggers. In 1890 Yosemite was declared a national park, with Mariposa added a few years later.

Mercifully, the Bachelor and the Three Graces have been left more or less to their own devices. (A simple fence protects them from all but their most ardent admirers.) Part of the reason for their elegance is that they are neither very large nor very old – as giant sequoias go. But the Bachelor and the Three Graces have still the bloom of youth: the russet-grey bark, the voluptuous curves, the mane of bright green needles. No one knows their age, but I should imagine that it's only about 700 years since they started to flirt together on this delightful hillside.

GRIZZLIES

A California song...
A chorus of dryads, fading, departing, or hamadryads departing,
A murmuring, fateful, giant voice, out of the earth and sky,
Voice of a mighty dying tree in the redwood forest dense.
Farewell my brethren,
Farewell O earth and sky, farewell ye neighbouring waters,
My time has ended, my term has come.

WALT WHITMAN, SONG OF THE REDWOOD-TREE

The Cedars They Turned into Totems

THERE'S A GOOD MOMENT IN Tolkien's *The Lord of the Rings* when the 'ents' – half-human trees of gigantic size – turn on Saruman, the evil wizard, and start to tear down his castle with their roots. Saruman had been cutting down trees, and the trees had had enough. If only we had a few ents around today! But in a sense we do. We have the western red cedar (*Thuja plicata*). No other tree combines such a monstrous shape with such astonishing size. No wonder the coast Indians of the Pacific chose the largest of them to carve into totem poles.

To the Indians this tree, whose aromatic red wood seemed immortal, supplied the sinews of peace and war: wigwams and war canoes and (from its roots) baskets and bowls and fishing gear. Unfortunately for the Indians – and the species itself – the tree was also excellent for building European houses. The newcomers hacked down the original cedar forests for 1000 miles along the rain-sodden coasts of the Pacific. Most of the trees today are youngsters. (To smell the tansy-like tang of an ancient cedar forest you must now go north of the Canadian border, and here, too, they are vanishing fast.) However, a few giant individuals have somehow survived. Most have found sanctuary in national parks close to the sea, especially on the western side of the Olympic Mountains in Washington State. I have chosen a contrasting pair for this book.

The Quinault Lake Cedar, with a volume of 17,650 cubic feet, has recently been recognized as the champion red cedar of the world. With Washington State's leading big-tree hunter, Bob Van Pelt, I climbed up the side of a small ravine to the spongy terrace of young western hemlock where the great cedar had secluded itself. Belatedly, this scrap of old-growth forest had been rescued from the loggers.

When you reach the terrace, the cedar confronts you like a gigantic grizzly bear – or rather like one of Tolkien's ents hell-bent on pulling down Saruman's castle. It is not a confrontation I should enjoy while alone on a moonlit walk. The tree is a grinning skeleton, with most of its bark gone, and a pair of lightless rooms, like burial chambers, hidden in its vast fetid trunk.

The Kalaloch Cedar, 30 miles away up the coast, is a great deal more welcoming. Fifth largest red cedar in the world, judged by volume, it is the biggest of all in girth – by a margin of six inches. A cheerful Gothic light filters through its mossy windows into its vaulted interior. Years ago an audacious hemlock seeded itself 20 feet up on the cedar's trunk and another followed. Now there are two full-grown hemlock spruce up there, extending their bony roots to the ground like flying buttresses.

Preceding page: THE QUINAULT LAKE RED CEDAR, WASHINGTON STATE. ONE OF TOLKIEN'S ENTS?

Above: THE RED CEDAR AT KALALOCH, WASHINGTON STATE – BIGGEST-GIRTHED IN THE WORLD
Opposite: DETAIL OF THE KALALOCH CEDAR. I FOUND IT A FRIENDLY CAVE

The Tree That Looks Like a Troll

THE SKYSCRAPER TREES OF AUSTRALIA are all species of eucalyptus: mountain ash (*E. regnans*) in New South Wales and Tasmania, karri (*E. diversicolor*)in Western Australia, brown-top stringybark (*E. obliqua)* and manna gum (*E. viminalis*) in Tasmania. All these species once produced champions well in excess of 300 feet high – and most experts would agree that one or two exceptional mountain ash exceeded 350 feet. Today there is not a single tree in Australia known to reach 300 feet. The loggers have made sure of that. Mercifully, all four species were widely distributed where rain was abundant, so numerous fine specimens of the next rank have been preserved.

If only one could say the same of the unfortunate red tingle. Hemmed in by karris in a few valleys close to the town of Walpole in Western Australia, the species (*Eucalyptus jacksonii*) was by far the rarest and thus the most vulnerable. The timber made excellent furniture. Today, I was told, only a handful of giant red tingles remain, and most of the largest have been ravaged by fire.

I drove down to Walpole one day in November 2001 expecting the worst. Belatedly, the state has given protection to some of the survivors. You can bounce along on a million-dollar walkway a hundred feet up in the forest at a place now styled 'Valley of the Giants'. But the giants are mostly karris. I could hardly find a single tingle for my lens – nothing at any rate that would stir the heart.

A few miles to the west I found a farm track leading to 'The Great Tingle'. It didn't look promising, but it was – a revelation. Old tingles are like trolls: brutal, ugly, magnificent creatures that can outlive the elegant karris by centuries. I left the car and tramped through a forest that would have inspired Tolkien. The troll ahead was the biggest. It was 65 feet in girth at breast height – much bigger in girth than any eucalyptus I had yet seen – and split by fire from head to toe. A great plume of branches grew from its head. Yet the bole was a vast cavern open to the sky. For the first time since coming to Australia I felt overwhelmed by the scale and power of the thing. Like Goethe standing below the great waterfall of the Rhine, I felt I was in the presence of the sublime.

Opposite: THE GIANT RED TINGLE NEAR WALPOLE, WESTERN AUSTRALIA. NOT MUCH LEFT FOR THE LOGGERS

Sherman v. Grant in the Sierras

PEOPLE SOMETIMES WONDER WHY the biggest tree in the world was called after William T. Sherman, the most brutal of the Union commanders in the American Civil War. I think they would get their answer if they came to Sequoia National Park, California, and looked at his namesake.

I stood there one dismal day in November, peering up at the 274-feet-high victorious general. As I watched him, a snow cloud descended and began to hide his monstrous upper arms. 'Each one of those branches,' said a local guide without much exaggeration, 'is bigger than any *tree* east of the Mississipi.'

Of all the hundreds of ancient giant sequoias, spread over 66 groves in the Sierra Nevada Mountains, this is the most brutal. Sherman's neighbours taper gently as they soar to the heavens. General Sherman himself, all 1500 tons of him, eyes you with the bluntness of a heavy tank in World War II (and, of course, that was another of the general's incarnations). To the observer from below, the trunk's 60-foot girth appears not to taper at all from a height of about 30 feet to 150 feet. (In fact it does taper but only by about 12 feet.) Everything about this brute is in character. His grizzled branches, mutilated by storms, protrude like giant stalks of broccoli. His broken head culminates in a 50-foot long jagged spike. If he could not claim the world championship for size, he could claim the prize for ugliness.

Compare the muscular curves of his northern neighbour – and rival – General Grant, the giant of King's Canyon National Park. Grant is certainly somewhat grizzled, as you'd expect from a veteran of more than a thousand winters. But he carries his vast size without apparent strain. His smooth, conical head and cinnamon-coloured upper trunk have somehow escaped the ravages of storms. His foliage falls like a bright green cascade. No wonder that in 1965, when President Lyndon B. Johnson was asked to nominate 'The Nation's Christmas Tree', he chose General Grant not General Sherman.

The rivalry between the two trees goes back a century and a half, and endangered the peace of two Californian counties. General Grant was discovered in 1862 and was clearly the biggest tree in what was to become King's Canyon National Park in Fresno County. General Sherman was discovered in 1879 and dominated what was to become Sequoia National Park in Tulare County. Which giant was the bigger giant? To avoid a new civil war the authorities agreed in 1921 to hire a team of surveyors and put the matter to arbitration. The result of careful measurements (confirmed by modern big-tree hunters with laser equipment) is rather surprising.

Neither tree is the tallest giant sequoia nor the biggest in girth. These honours go to lesser known giant sequoias in the Sierras. But Sherman's 274-feet height compared to Grant's 266 feet, and Grant's 91-feet girth compared to Sherman's 85 feet make Grant the bigger (though not the biggest of all) judged by the American Forestry Association's complicated system of points normally used for judging champion trees.* But Sherman's 55,040-cubic-feet volume is greater than Grant's 47,930 cubic feet. This means that if the champ's the one with most volume, then Sherman's the champ – indeed the biggest living thing in the whole world.

I think Grant was robbed.

* The AFA, embarrassed by this controversy, decided to suspend its normal points system in this case, allowing Sherman to win.

Opposite: GENERAL GRANT, THE RUNNER-UP. WAS HE ROBBED?

At the Feet of the Emperor

WHEN I TOLD A JAPANESE FRIEND IN TOKYO that I had come to Japan to sit at the feet of some remarkable trees, he smiled and said: 'Ah, if only you could get to Yaku Island and sit at the feet of Daio Sugi'.

Daio Sugi means 'Emperor Cedar', but as there's another ancient cedar of that name, he's usually known as Jomon Sugi ('The Old Cedar'). Under that name he has become one of the cult trees of Japan. He is the oldest, the biggest (50 feet in girth, with no taper for the next 40 feet) and the grimmest specimen of the Japanese cedar (*Cryptomeria japonica*) in the country.

For centuries this was the species that clothed the bony chain of mountains along half the length of Japan, and supplied the fragrant logs that built the shrines and palaces of Edo (Tokyo) and Kyoto. Most of the ancient trees on the mainland were felled long ago (except for a few noble specimens in Shinto shrines, and one famous avenue leading to Nikko). The old-growth forests are now cherished only in paintings and woodcuts. But on remote Yaku Island – mountainous, subtropical and 700 miles south-west of Tokyo – Jomon Sugi eluded the loggers. Thirty years ago Yaku Island was declared a World Heritage site and Jomon Sugi (with a few other giant cedars and a treasure chest of deer and monkeys) was saved for posterity.

The island was hooded by rain-clouds when I landed there in a small turbo-prop late one November afternoon. But two days later, in steaming sunshine, I set off for Jomon Sugi. We followed a narrow-gauge railway line built by the loggers years before. The climb presented no problems. But I had some uneasy moments when crossing gorges. I had to walk along a slippery plank at the centre of the old railway line, without the ghost of a hand-rail, trying not to see, through the gaps in the sleepers, the river foaming hundreds of feet below.

After a mere three and a half hours we were astonished to see Jomon Sugi looking down at us through the mist. And look down he does: a grim titan of a tree, rising from the spongy ground more like rock than timber, his vast muscular arms extended above the tangle of young cedars and camphor trees.

With a volume of about 10,000 cubic feet, Jomon Sugi, the Emperor Cedar, is certainly an imperial giant, not only the biggest conifer in Japan but bigger than any, I think, in Europe. Japanese scientists, making ring-counts from his branches, reckon he's over 2000 years old. Could we know more? I sat at his feet in the mist and wondered whether any one would dare ask him his age by boring a hole through his trunk and counting the rings. Perish the thought! You do not ask a god-emperor his age.

Opposite: JOMON SUGI, EMPEROR OF YAKU ISLAND – BIGGEST, OLDEST AND GRIMMEST CEDAR IN JAPAN.

FOR FEAR OF LITTLE MEN

*I fear those grey, old men of Moccas, those grey gnarled,
low-browed, knock-kneed, bowed... deformed,
hunchbacked, misshapen oak men that stand waiting
and watching century after century.*

FRANCIS KILVERT ON THE MOCCAS OAKS, DIARY 1876

Preceding page: A JUNIPER
STOICALLY FACES THE WIND 6000
FEET UP IN THE TAURUS
MOUNTAINS, SOUTHERN TURKEY

Pages 52–3: WESTERN JUNIPER ON
GRANITE AT YOSEMITE NATIONAL
PARK, CALIFORNIA

No Love Lost Between the Brothers

Above: THE TURKISH VARIETY
OF THE CEDAR OF LEBANON
SHARES THE MOUNTAINS WITH
THE JUNIPERS

Opposite: THIS BROTHER
IS THE EXHIBITIONIST

GARDENERS HAVE NO FEAR OF DWARFS – indeed, they court them. Under the botanical name *nana* (dwarf), countless varieties of tree have taken on an extra exotic form, cheerfully adapting their roots to the smallest, most domestic garden. And they still leave room, if you need it, for a concrete gnome.

Out in the wild, dwarfs have a more masterful air. You can sense they are a power to be reckoned with, like the dwarfs in the best fairy stories (Tolkien's Gimli, not Disney's seven cuddly old men) with nothing small about their virtues – especially their capacity for endurance.

I was reminded of this air of mastery one day in autumn 2001 when I stumbled on a grove of ancient junipers (*Juniperus excelsa*) growing on white limestone scree 6000 feet up in the Taurus Mountains of south-west Turkey. Some of these junipers were mere lumpish green bushes, like ordinary junipers of the common species (*Juniperus communis*) you find sprawling on hillsides all over the northern hemisphere. (Don't say a word against juniper bushes. Without their pungent blue berries how could we flavour our gin?) Others were huge trees by any standard, nearly 20 feet in girth, with gnarled and twisted trunks. Many of these were about 1000 years old, I should reckon, based on ring-counts taken of ancient junipers growing in North America. But it was the dwarfs, not the giants or the bushes, that caught my eye – in particular two powerful dwarfs growing on the most exposed flank of the mountain.

Both had been bleached white by the elements: ice-storms in January, oven-hot winds at midsummer. And, of course, their growth had been stunted by the same elements. But in other ways they presented a singular contrast. The smaller tree resembled an oriental carving in ivory. Storms had skinned the trunk, leaving its sinews exposed. Only a small artery of living bark connected its roots with its branches. But its carriage was upright and defiant. The larger tree seemed like a complete stranger. Storms had ripped off part of its trunk. Yet it was not content simply to survive. It kicked up its heels in a wild Turkish dance.

The oddest thing was that these two trees were growing on the same stony hillside a few yards from each other. They were brothers perhaps, self-sown from the same parent trees. But not, of course, genetically the same. And I suppose that was why they behaved so differently.

There seemed to be no love lost between the pair. I feel every sympathy for the stoic brother stuck with that ridiculous exhibitionist.

Opposite: WESTERN JUNIPERS
RISING FROM THE GRANITE 8000
FEET UP IN YOSEMITE NATIONAL
PARK, CALIFORNIA

Bury Me in a Tomb of Granite

A YEAR BEFORE THAT TRIP TO THE TAURUS MOUNTAINS, I found myself driving along an icy road towards the Tioga Pass, over 9000 feet up in the eastern corner of Yosemite National Park, California. I wondered if I would be able to get through. The pass is normally closed by snow about the beginning of November, and it was now 3 November. I was lucky – and not only to escape a 400-mile detour around the Sierra Nevada. My eye was caught by a dwarf western juniper (*Juniperus occidentalis*) growing near the summit of the pass. This type of American juniper is known for its ability to survive arid, inhospitable uplands. But in its choice of a home here it seemed to have taken perversity to extremes. The subalpine firs and Sierra pines that dominated these dry, upper slopes of the mountain were living off the fat of the land compared to this eccentric juniper. It had forced its way up between two blocks of granite like a man pushing his way out of the grave at the Last Judgement. And it was stunted by the arctic wind as well as by the granite. Why on earth choose this icy graveyard for a home?

The mystery only deepened as I looked at other junipers scattered about the slopes. One had chosen to curl up beside a huge boulder in the most exposed part of the granite pavement. Its claws scrabbled between the cracks (see page 00). Others had chosen agonizingly uncomfortable positions in successive shelves of granite on the canyon ahead. Some had every appearance of great age – over 1000 years, I would assume – as their trunks were largely decayed. All bore the signs of extreme stress, self-inflicted apparently.

I wondered if these stunted dwarfs were the remnants of a healthy forest of junipers that once crowned these arid slopes. Had the rest gone to the sawmills? (Juniper makes princely furniture, as it is as hard and fine-grained as yew and smells like incense.) I asked some friends who knew this eastern part of Yosemite, and I was told there was no mystery. For once the loggers were not to blame. No, this was the Sierra's timber-line – the place where the forest ends and the raw mountain begins. At this level all trees are on sufferance and seize their chance where they can. Lower down, the juniper is handicapped by its small size, its thin, inflammable bark and a passion for daylight. To survive among the bullying pines and firs it must fawn and flatter, twisting itself like a hunchback jester. But up here, in its icy tomb of granite, the jester becomes king.

The Golden Cup of Joshua Tree Park

Left: A CANYON LIVE
OAK HAPPY AMONG
THE RATTLESNAKES
AT JOSHUA NATIONAL
PARK, CALIFORNIA

I HAVE ALWAYS ADMIRED the great evergreen oaks of the Deep South of the USA, known there as 'live oaks'. Covered in Spanish moss and haunted by fruit-bats, they are as much symbols of the steamy world of the slave-owners as their crumbling ante-bellum houses, and many are a good deal older. Imagine my surprise, then, to find a perfect specimen of a live oak growing wild in the burning desert of California, in the Joshua Tree National Park, only just over the hill, so to speak, from Death Valley. True, it was a different species of live oak – canyon live oak, also known as golden cup oak – *Quercus chrysolepis* as opposed to the common live oak, *Quercus virginina*. The oven heat of summer had clearly stunted the tree. But there was something miraculous about its presence there in the desert, undaunted by the yellow rocks the shape of enormous pebbles. My guidebook said that, if I was lucky, I might see at least one of the three kinds of rattlesnake that make this their home: sidewinder, speckled and Mojave. No doubt they were watching me from that group of wizened bushes. Around the tree crouched brittlebush and creosote and drought-tormented specimens of the same canyon live oak. The tree itself rose serenely 30 feet into the sky, fully mature (you could see that from its rounded head) and perfectly proportioned.

What was its secret? I should like to be there in March, when it sometimes rains and the desert glows with Indian paintbrush and desert dandelion. I bet there's a hidden spring under the tree that fills up at that time of year. I should also like to see the tree in summer when its acorns ripen, for it is their woolly golden cups that have given the tree its Arthurian name.

Opposite: A CYPRESS ON
THE ROCKS AT MONTEREY,
CALIFORNIA

Overleaf: CYPRESSES ON
THE BEACH AT MONTEREY,
CALIFORNIA. DID I DO
THEM AN INJUSTICE?

The Beachcomber of Monterey

IN MY EARLIER BOOK, *Meetings with Remarkable Trees*, I described the Monterey cypress (*Cupressus macrocarpa*) somewhat fancifully as 'the tree that longs to get away from home'. I was struck by the paradox that this tree grows better almost anywhere than in its native home at Monterey, California. I'm afraid I did it an injustice. To tell the truth, I had only read about Monterey in those days. When I had the good fortune to go there myself and stretch my legs on its delicious beach, I realized the wild cypresses are perfectly happy to do so too.

True, the trees are stunted by the wind that blows straight from New Zealand, 6000 miles away across the howling waves of the Pacific. Only two small native populations have survived this eternal battering. The tallest tree is hardly more than 50 feet high, and most have been sculpted by the wind to form grotesque bushes. But try sowing the seed of the Monterey cypress anywhere except at Monterey! It will reach 120 feet high with a girth to match. That's nothing for a Monterey cypress in Cornwall or Ireland. Even in my own garden, where frost regularly turns our best magnolia blooms to rags, a Monterey cypress towers above the humble native pines.

Why did this wild cypress never leave Monterey? In fact, it did once and colonized great swathes of the temperate world. This is the record of its ancient pedigree that you can read from fossilized leaves. Then, roughly a million years ago, the first of four ice ages began, and the giants of the Pacific – red cedar, redwood, giant sequoia, Douglas fir and Monterey cypress – started the first of their four temporary retreats to safety in southern California and Mexico. When it was all over, 12,000 years ago, and the great trees were safely home again in the icy Sierra Nevada and the rain-sodden coasts to the north, the Monterey cypress was missing. No one can say why. Palaeobotany is often as foggy as the coast of California. At any rate, the cypress stayed put, very sensibly, basking on the beach at Monterey.

IN BONDAGE

Little laurel trees, your roots can find
No mountain, yet your leaves extend
Beyond your own world into mine
Perennial wands, unfolding in my thought
The budding evergreen of time.

KATHLEEN RAINE, THE TREES IN TUBS

Preceding page: IN BONDAGE: A WESTERN JUNIPER BONSAIED AT THE HUNTINGDON GARDEN, CALIFORNIA. IS A LITTLE GENTLE TORTURE THE SECRET OF LONGEVITY?

Opposite: ANOTHER BONSAIED DWARF THAT MIGHT OUTLIVE THE GIANTS – A JAPANESE ZELKOVA

Tie up My Feet, Darling, and I'll Live for Ever

ONE OF THE ODD RESULTS of the opening up of Japan to foreigners, after the fall of the Shogunate in 1867, was the craze for bonsai. This fashion for dwarfing trees by constricting their feet in small pots originated in China, and had reached Japan by at least as early as the 14th century. From the first it had its detractors. A famous satirist, Kenko Yoshida (1283–1351) wrote: 'To appreciate and find pleasure in curiously curved potted trees is to love deformity.'

However, there was no stopping the wave of bonsai mania that swept Japan in the late 19th and early 20th centuries. No doubt it was a reaction to a parallel craze for everything Western, and a return to one of the most Japanese of arts that seemed to make a giant of the artist who practised it. At any rate, the new craze for bonsai sent people scouring the mountains for natural dwarfs, hunting for Sargent's junipers on Mount Ishizuchi, for cut-leaf cherries on Mount Fuji and so on. These natural dwarfs were trees of the wilderness, twisted by the rocks, stunted by wind and ice. Artificial dwarfs were trained to imitate them, and soon, after a few years of imprisonment in small pots, they out-dwarfed and out-wildernessed them.

I have chosen these two elegant bonsai from the oriental section of the Huntingdon Garden near Los Angeles,

California. In fact, one is an American native, artificially dwarfed in the Japanese style: a western juniper (*Juniperus occidentalis*). The other is a Japanese zelkova (*Zelkova serrata*). I photographed them in November, when the beech's leaves were turning, and a fallen leaf from a nearby Japanese maple gave scale to the juniper.

Bonsai gardeners rightly pride themselves on their patience and artistry. The tree is imprisoned in a small pot or tray to make it small and beautiful, rather as Chinese ladies of fashion used to have their feet bound. But here the analogy fails. By contrast with the Chinese ladies, who were effectively crippled by foot-binding, confining the bonsai sets it free from the constraints of ageing, and gives it a kind of perpetual youth. Every couple of years, its older roots are clipped off and its ancient trunk manicured. The stress forces it to throw out juvenile roots and shoots. Bonsai experts believe that a bonsai might become virtually immortal – or at any rate live for thousands of years – if properly disciplined.

I am reminded of the story of the admirer who greeted Max Beerbohm, then a boyish-looking, elderly man of letters, with the words: 'Max, you have found the secret of perpetual youth.' To which Beerbohm replied sadly: 'No, I have found the secret of perpetual old age.'

CHAPTER THREE
METHUSELAHS

THE LIVING AND THE DEAD

*...the oldest pines have in a certain sense been dying for two millenniums
or more. They now possess only a narrow strip of their once complete
bark and the growing tissue beneath it. True, the dying-back of this
life-line is exceedingly slow, and several of them seem good for at least
five centuries still. But they probably cannot live much more.*

DR EDMUND SCHULMAN, DISCOVERER OF 'METHUSELAHS WALK',
IN THE NATIONAL GEOGRAPHIC

The Old Man
and the Mountain

IT WOULD BE HARD TO IMAGINE an eerier setting than the bony, bleached, lunar slopes 10,000 feet up in the White Mountains of California, where Dr Edmund Schulman found the oldest trees in the world.

Six thousand feet below, the once-green Owens Valley, robbed of its water by the City of Los Angeles, stares blankly up at you. Four thousand feet above, and 20 miles away, as a crow would fly across the Owens Valley, the snow-capped peaks of the Sierra Nevada dazzle the eye with their spires and battlements.

And here in the grove of bristlecone pines that Dr Schulman christened Methuselah Walk, is the Old Man himself, at over 4600 years, the oldest living tree known to science.

When Schulman began his study of bristlecone pines (*Pinus longaeva*) people still believed that the biggest trees in the world, the giant sequoias, were also the oldest. Thousands of giant sequoias had been felled by the loggers, and in many cases the rings could still be easily counted all the way to the centre (the wood is almost rot-proof), dating some trees over 3000 years old.

Schulman made his amazing discoveries in the mid-1950s. Using a Swedish tree-borer, three feet long and only the thickness of a pencil, he took a series of radial cores from the bristlecone pines. Then, in his laboratory, he counted the tree rings under a microscope. Seventeen trees proved to be over 4000 years old and still alive – in a fashion.

Paradoxically, Schulman found no link between the size of the ancient trees and their age. Instead, longevity in trees seems linked to stress. (If only the same could be said of humans. Poor Dr Schulman died exhausted at 49.) The oldest bristlecone pines have chosen the most stressful climate imaginable: in winter buried in snow or wind-blasted by ice crystals, in spring and summer parched by the sun, with nothing to drink except melting snow, and only a few weeks when growth is possible. So stress slows down the tree's clock to the absolute minimum necessary for life (stress does the same for the bonsai, but by forcing the bonsai to produce juvenile roots and shoots it would supposedly make it immortal). In fact, the oldest bristlecones live in the twilight between life and death. The main trunk dies several thousand years before the last of its branches, whose life finally hangs by a thread – the thread of bark attached to the roots.

Schulman's advances on the frontiers of dendrochronology (he and his successors sampled 9000-year-old dead wood here in the White Mountains) gave a serious jolt to archaeologists

as it proved they had wrongly calibrated the scale for carbon dating by hundreds of years. The so-called 3500-year-old megaliths of Ireland, for example, proved 500 years older than that. There was also one disastrous result of Schulman's work. A geography student in Utah thought he would find a bristlecone even older than Schulman's Old Man. And he did. He borrowed a tree-borer and found a tree in the Snake Mountains of Nevada and Utah that could be dated 4900 years old. But the borrowed tree-borer snapped off in the tree. Incredibly, the local ranger gave him permission to cut down the tree to rescue the tree-borer. Today, all that remains of the tree that *was* the oldest tree in the world is a slice of the trunk on show in a gambling saloon in Nevada.

I climbed the mountain leading to Schulman's Methuselah Walk one icy day in October 2000. It was no picnic: a five-mile yomp (as the Paras used to say) across frozen scree, carrying a 30-lb Linhof camera and tripod, and panting in the thin air 10,000 feet up. Of course, it was irresistible. When the moon came up over the twisted corpses of dead and dying trees, I must have looked like one of the Two Men Contemplating the Moon in the painting by Caspar David Friedrich.

But which old tree was the Old Man himself? Very sensibly, the authorities keep his identity secret. I have my suspicions. But I shall take no chances with geography students, and keep my suspicions to myself.

The Kvilleken and the Green Man

I SPLASHED THROUGH SOUTHERN SWEDEN, pursued by summer squalls, across a pleasant landscape striped with young forests of spruce and pine, and dotted with half-hidden lakes. I had come to pay my respects to the common oak (*Quercus robur*) with the largest girth in all Europe. To my surprise, I found the champion growing in humble enough soil. He rose to greet me from a boulder-strewn paddock, close by a modern farmhouse with a red-tiled roof. The farm didn't seem to give much of a living these days. The cattle sheds were half derelict, and elegantly twisted junipers were invading the small fields enclosed by forests of pine. But the owners are making a go of it by giving home-made teas to the trickle of Swedish tourists who come to see the Kvilleken, the great oak of Kvill.

As a champion he wins only on points. This is not an oak to knock you down with its heroic size or its God-given looks. He is the broadest oak in Europe – 50 feet around, measured at breast height, the official height for measuring girth. But above that level he tapers rapidly. I don't think he was ever enormous in volume, like giant oaks I've seen in Britain, France and Germany. But I'm sure he was once beautiful. Today he is a noble ruin, hollow from head to toe, with a rusty chain round his neck. It must be decades since storms tore off most of his upper limbs, and well-meaning experts tried to patch him up with steel chains. In the long run this kind of help is usually disastrous, as the chains bite into the flesh of growing trees. Yet, despite it all, the Kvilleken is alive and well and breeding. In August I saw acorns on some of the branches, and they looked healthy. His branches were well furnished with leaves, which murmured in the wind – approvingly, I hope – as I set up my camera to take his portrait.

And do I deceive myself, or didn't I catch the cheerful figure of the Green Man, the pagan symbol of fertility, lurking in the hollows of his trunk? (See the photograph.)

What is astonishing about the Kvilleken is that he has grown so large and survived so long. I would expect him to be about 750 years old, about the same age as the Chapel-Oak of Allouville in Normandy. But this poor stony soil is so different from Allouville's. Traditionally, oaks were used to value the quality of land. The finer the oak, the richer and deeper the soil. The Kvilleken has grown fat on a pittance.

Could the answer be, quite simply, that the great oaks on the good soils of Sweden were cut down long ago, and the land turned over to farming or forestry? The Kvilleken survived because the original acorn had fallen on stony ground. Long life to the Green Man!

Parsifal and the Holy Grail

Opposite:
THE WOLFRAMSLINDE AT
RIED, BAVARIA. WAS THIS
WHERE WOLFRAM WROTE
PARSIFAL?

ALMOST EXACTLY THE SAME GIRTH as the Kvilleken – 50 feet around – a huge, ancient, hollow lime tree straddles the village green at Ried, three miles from Koetzing in Lower Bavaria. Like the Kvilleken, this large-leaved lime (*Tilia platyphyllos*) must be the champion tree of its species. But it is very much more than a champion. It is one of the most beautiful trees I have encountered.

Trees, like people, rarely combine the age of Methuselah with the beauty of Helen of Troy. The great lime of Ried is a radiant exception. I photographed it one morning in August 2000 as the sun began to light up the fountain of young branches springing from the ancient, hollow trunk. And what a trunk! All it needs is an early Renaissance dragon, painted by Uccello, lying in wait for the princess in the blue dress.

Local historians believe that the tree is a thousand years old. This is just possible, I think. Lime wood is too soft to be very durable (its softness made it the wood favoured by Grinling Gibbons for carving flowers and fruit and goddesses) but the tree has an astonishing power of renewal. You have only to look at the way it has re-grown its head, torn off by a storm about 30 years ago. An ancient oak would never have been able to summon the energy to perform such a feat. Other long-lived species – plane and sweet chestnut – would have reacted by growing new trunks beside the old one. The lime seems to re-invent itself without effort.

For more than a century this tree has carried the courtly name of 'Wolframslinde' – the lime of Wolfram von Eschenbach, the medieval troubadour who wrote the original German version of *Parsifal*. He stayed for long periods at the nearby castle of Haidstein, where he fell in love with its irresistible chatelaine, Markgraefin von Haidstein. Many of his epic poems, including his *Parzival*, were apparently composed in her honour – some of them, so Bavarians like to believe, while sitting under this lime tree.

I think I was wrong about Uccello. It would be a mistake to paint a dragon for this tree, lying in wait for the princess in the blue dress. What we need is the Wagnerian hero Parsifal, the knight who is searching for the Holy Grail. Your quest is over, Parsifal! The Holy Grail is buried over there, at the foot of the tree.

They Say You Knew Julius Caesar

VAL D'ULTIMO, THE 'FINAL VALLEY' of the Italian Tirol (Ultental to the German-speaking majority), is as pretty as it looks on postcards. Even in late June the Alpine meadows sparkle with wildflowers. After the hurly-burly of the plains below, your ears re-tune to the soft voices of the forests, the murmur of the bright green larch, the rustle of the dark green spruce, broken only by the childlike sound of cowbells.

I drove up the valley from Merano one delightful summer day in 2001. Italian experts, whose opinion I respected, had told me that the three oldest larches in Europe grew near San Gertruda, the last village in the valley. Their precise age was known, and it came to the astonishing figure of 2085, making them contemporaries with Julius Caesar, and thus by far the oldest trees of any species in Europe for which we had an accurate date.

I found the three larches huddled together dominating a steep hillside, a hundred yards above an old, wooden-roofed farmhouse with cowsheds and barns. The people of San Gertruda are proud of their *Urlaerchen* (primeval larches), and showed me the track. But old trees are a rarity in this alpine landscape of small farms and state forests. These three brother larches were spared the axe, in order to protect the farm from avalanches. Originally there were four brothers. About 70 years ago, the fourth blew down – or was cut down or was burnt down. At any rate, the rings on the stump were counted by someone, whose name is now forgotten, and the total came to 2015. So this is the origin of the pedigree of the three surviving brothers. Add 70 years and, hey presto, you get 2085.

The largest Urlaerche, a huge tree with a bole nearly 20 feet round, is the most vigorous. Although its trunk looks at least partly hollow, its head is still throwing out delicate young branches. The second brother has lost part of its crown. A young larch, no doubt one of its own seedlings, has settled in its lap, like a kangaroo baby in its mother's pouch. The third brother is the smallest and the most decayed. I sat in the cave of its trunk looking up at the blue sky as if I was looking up a chimney.

Are these hollow old trees really as old as it is claimed? Or have the experts been fooled by a tall story from the mountains? I am puzzled by this story of the fourth larch, on which the claim for dating them rests. I find too many gaps – you could say hollows – in it. Who was the man who counted the rings? Did he really count them in 1930? Why did he leave no written record? And if the fourth tree was hollow, like its three brothers, how did he count its rings?

I have seen old larches in other parts of Europe. Three hundred years is a great age for a larch as its wood rots faster than the wood of oaks, sweet chestnut or (above all) yews.

I think the three brothers are astonishingly old. They are genuine wonders. But my guess is that they are closer in date to Cesare Borgia than to Julius Caesar – about a quarter of the age attributed to them.

Right: THE THREE LARCHES OF VAL D'ULTIMO. NOT EXACTLY THE SAME AGE AS JULIUS CAESAR

Justice under the Oak

Above: THE FEME-EICHE AT ERLE, WESTPHALIA. JUSTICE OAK OR RAVEN OAK?

Opposite: DETAIL OF FEME-EICHE'S MENACING BRANCHES

IN 1838, WHEN JOHN LOUDON, the Scottish encyclopedist, published his magisterial eight-volume work on British trees, *Arboretum et Fruticetum Britannicum*, he included some astonishing information about European trees. In writing about Germany, Loudon quoted a 16th-century writer, Googe, who described an 'oke' in Westphalia which was 130 feet from the ground to the 'neerest bowe'. There was another 'oke' with a girth of over 90 feet.

These trees sound as if they would have made an excellent home for unicorns. What is certain is that no European tree exists today approaching that size in height or girth. However, Westphalia, in north-west Germany, does produce noble oaks. One of the most famous is the *Feme-Eiche* (Justice Oak) at Erle in Westphalia.

Some historians believe this tree was originally a pagan shrine dedicated to Wotan, as it's still called by old people the *Raben-Eiche* (Raven Oak), and the raven was sacred to Wotan. In the 13th century the Emperor instituted local courts in Westphalia, called *Feme*, where his opponents could be tried in secret by deputies he had appointed. The tree, still associated perhaps with the dark rites of Wotan, was made to serve as a secret court of justice. The sinister practice lapsed, and by the 19th century the Justice Oak, now completely hollow, was considered a suitable place for celebrations: in 1819 the Crown Prince paraded 30 fully equipped infantrymen inside the tree.

I visited Erle on a sunny morning in July 2000. It was an eerie experience, although the tree is now marooned in an unromantic suburb. In 1892 the oak measured 41 feet around its sagging 'stomach'. It was then reckoned 1200 years old and the oldest oak in the whole of Germany. Today its stomach is no longer there to be measured. The tree is a tripod of tattered bark held up on wooden props. Yet the oak still carries a head of twisted branches, which bear green leaves and fertile acorns. And it still holds some pagan menace in its skull-like trunk and claw-like arms. It is not a place where I would choose to be tried for my life.

Did the Dragon Grow a New Head?

I WAS MOURNING THE LOSS of the great dragon tree of Orotava on the north coast of Tenerife, famous for centuries after the conquistadors seized the island for Spain during the early Renaissance. Then I acquired a 160-year-old engraving that made my pulse race.

Compare the engraving of the dragon tree (near right) with the photograph of the dragon tree (opposite). Do they show the same tree?

Let me explain the puzzle. The engraving of the Orotava tree was published about 1840. My photograph was taken at Icod, near Orotava, in February 2002, when I visited the tree, now one of the main attractions of the island. There was an earlier engraving of the Orotava tree published in 1809 by Baron von Humboldt, based on earlier sketches. Humboldt had returned from his travels with tales of the great dragon tree of Orotava, which he estimated at 6000 years old. What is certain is that Humboldt's engraving was wildly inaccurate, although the tree was certainly enormous: reputedly 60 feet high and 35 feet in girth at breast height. My 1840 engraving looks accurate and is uncannily like the photograph. Are these the same outbuildings, the same garden dotted with palm trees, the same jagged mountains across the valley? As for the dragon tree itself, it seems much the same – a crumbling monster in either case, with a gash across its throat in the engraving, and a huge scar across its throat in the photograph.

The puzzle was that the first tree – Humboldt's – blew down, according to all accounts, in a storm in the late 1860s. So the tree I captured on my lens at Icod must be a different one. Or had the tree, like a hydra, been able to grow a new head after the storm? This was a thrilling – I almost said *heady* – hypothesis.

The tree at Icod, at any rate, is a 30-foot-girthed marvel, although, strictly speaking, not a tree. Like all dragon trees, its 'trunk' has no concentric rings under the bark, and is just a bundle of roots that have tied themselves together like piping. This species *(Dracaena draco)* of Tenerife, other Canary islands and North Africa, is one of 60 species of this romantic genus. There are dragon cousins in Socotra and

southern Africa. All species share the blood-red sap that, with the claw-like branches, gave the tree its name.

How long do they live? Poor Humboldt made himself a laughing stock with his guess that the tree was 6000 years old – earlier than the supposed biblical date for Creation. Modern botanists say that 600 years would be about the limit for this kind of Methuselah. But *did* Humboldt's tree grow a new head, and was it still there to pose for my camera?

I did some more research on my return from Tenerife, and here is the answer. Humboldt's tree was at Villa Orotava, three miles east of the town of that name. Icod is 10 miles to the west. You can't win every time.

Above: THE DRAGON TREE, AT OROTAVA, TENERIFE, DRAWN IN 1819. *Opposite:* THE DRAGON TREE AT ICOD, TENERIFE TODAY

SHRINES

A tree is a wonderful living organism...
it even gives shade to those who wield an axe
to cut it down.

BUDDHA

(INSCRIBED AT THE GATE OF A FOREST RESERVE AT KANDY, SRI LANKA)

First a Staff, Then a Leaning Tower

GO AND STAND UNDER THE ANCIENT CYPRESS in the cloister of the Franciscan church at Verucchio, five miles inland from Rimini, on the east coast of Italy. It's a leaning tower of a tree, but perfectly safe for visitors. Thirty years ago it was attacked by a hurricane which left it leaning at a menacing angle. But in December 2000 a local building firm generously brought along a crane and put it on crutches: three 30-feet-long steel tubes safely bolted to the floor of the cloister.

The tree (*C. sempervirens*) is not a giant by any standard, as it's less than 10 feet in girth. But it's one of the oldest cypresses in Europe, and one of the few with a noble pedigree. St Francis of Assisi planted it himself in about 1200. This was the legend I was told by the convent guest-master, Brother Michael. Eight hundred years! It may seem only the blinking of an eye to one of the 4000-year-old bristlecone pines of California. But in Europe it's a long lifetime for a tree, even the kinds with the most durable wood, such as oaks, sweet chestnuts and cypresses. Brother Michael, I believe the legend. The tree looks the part: an ageing aristocrat, still gamely breeding (notice the branches are full of cones), although now on crutches, with ribs showing through the green robe.

High in the dead branches of the tree a pair of pigeons, the symbol of St Francis, begin their evening chant. Brother Michael takes me across to the church to see the fresco of the saint planting the cypress in 1200. (The fresco itself looks fairly modern, but perhaps it's a copy of an earlier one.) Brother Michael explains how St Francis came here to found a new convent, and his helpers began to gather wood for a fire. St Francis threw on the fire his own staff, a freshly cut branch of cypress. Next morning the fire had burnt to ashes but the staff was miraculously green. 'All right,' said the saint, 'if you don't want to burn, then grow.' And he planted his staff in what was to be the centre of the new cloister.

The convent here, like the tree, has seen more prosperous days. Once the community was 40 strong. Now, as Catholicism in Italy has ebbed away, it's down to four. But Brother Michael seems a happy man. Handsome and dark-skinned (he says his father was a Turk from Albania), he explains that there may be only four of them now in Verucchio but there are 23,000 Franciscans worldwide. He picks me some figs from the orchard, and offers to enrol me for a week's retreat as soon as I can spare the time. A week under the shadow of that noble tree. What could be more refreshing?

Preceding page: ST FRANCIS' CYPRESS AT VERUCCHIO, NORTHERN ITALY, NOW 800 YEARS OLD. 'IF YOU DON'T WANT TO BURN, THEN GROW'

Opposite: DETAIL OF ST FRANCIS' CYPRESS. PIGEONS ARE APPROPRIATE

How They Saved the Chapel Oak

WHEN IS A TREE NOT A TREE? Answer: when it's a building. The Chêne-Chapelle (Chapel Oak) of Allouville, 30 miles north-west of Rouen, has been famous in France since the late 17th century. In 1696 the local *curé*, M. l'Abbé du Detroit, built a chapel in the interior, complete with an altar for saying mass, and a room for a hermit on the floor above. The chapel was formally dedicated to Our Lady of Peace. Soon it was a place of pilgrimage: especially on 15 August, the Feast of the Assumption of the Virgin. But in 1793, these sacred associations nearly proved fatal. By now the Revolution had become the Terror. The local communards had been authorized – like the Red Guards of Mao's China two centuries later – to root out all trace of organized religion. In high spirits, they burnt down the presbytery, then marched off to deal with the tree, shouting drunkenly (according to an eyewitness):

'To the Great Oak! Let's burn that *niche d'oraisons*!'

With great presence of mind, the local schoolmaster, Jean-Baptiste Bonheur, attached a large notice to the wall nearby: 'Temple of Reason'. And the tree was saved.

Since then the tree has suffered the usual fate of hollow common oaks (*Quercus robur*). Its head was shattered by a thunderbolt in the early 19th century. Its internal wounds, natural and man-made, suppurated. Most of the bark peeled off the east side. But help, of a kind, was never short. The dead top was crowned with a turret and a cross. Bark was replaced with a protective coat of oak shingles, capping the end of each great branch that fell. Inside, the Lady chapel was restored in 1853–4 (for which the Empress Eugénie presented a simple wooden statue of the Virgin), and the hermit's cell on the upper floor was converted to a Calvary chapel. In October 1854, the Archbishop of Rouen blessed the newly restored chapels with a *Te Deum* and a hymn written especially for the occasion:

L'auteur de la nature
A construit sans marteau
D'un monument nouveau
Les murs et la toiture.

Ce joli sanctuaire
Cet autel vénéré
A Marie est dressé
Dans l'arbre séculaire.

A hundred and fifty years later I stood and marvelled at how well the inside of the 'secular tree' looks today. In the early 1990s a new generation of restorers lavished care on the monument. The octagonal lower chapel has been refitted with linenfold panelling, strips of mirror glass to bring more light into the tree and a Gothic boss at the hub of the octagon. Eugénie's statue of the Virgin greets one from the altar. I climbed the staircase to the upper chapel – certainly too elegant, these days, for a hermit.

But outside, the tree continues on its inexorable decline. No one has any document to enable us to date it, but I would guess, from the fact it was already hollow 300 years ago, that it's now at least 750 years old. (The official age is '1200' years old, which would make it older than any known oak in the world. I doubt it.) Extreme old age is a painful time for trees – as it is for the rest of us. The latest restorers have corrected some of the errors of their predecessors (removing the iron bars tormenting it), given the tree a new coat of shingles and propped it up on two huge steel crutches. I admire their benevolence. But I hope that, when the life of the Chapel Oak becomes unendurable, it will be allowed to die in dignity.

Opposite: THE CHAPEL OAK AT ALLOUVILLE, NORMANDY, BOLTED, CABLED AND SHINGLED

Opposite: A YOUNG BO TREE SCRAMBLING UP THE WALLS AT ANURADHAPURA, SRI LANKA

Overleaf: THE ANCIENT BO TREE AT ANURADHAPURA, SRI LANKA, REVERED BY BUDDHISTS SINCE THE 2ND CENTURY BC. A WORSHIPPER (RIGHT) CLIMBS THE STAIRS TO THE TREE WITH A LOTUS AS AN OFFERING

The Tree from the Tree Where Buddha Sat

IN JANUARY 2000, Sri Lanka was in the throes of civil war. Tamil Tigers had seized part of the north of the island. Tamil suicide bombers had attacked targets as far south as the capital, Colombo. I was anxious to see the great Bo tree at Anuradhapura, in the north-central part of the island. This is, by any standard, the most revered tree in the entire world. For its pedigree goes back in an unbroken succession to a cutting from the actual fig tree under which Buddha found enlightenment in the 6th century BC. But was it madness to make a pilgrimage to the tree during a murderous war?

Friends in Colombo said there was no problem. It was true that the Tigers, who are Hindu, had tried to blow up the tree as a symbol of Buddhist oppression. But the government forces had now taken the situation in hand. January would be a perfect month for a visit.

I set off with a daredevil friend in a local taxi. If you survive a day's driving in Sri Lanka, terrorism holds no fears for you. We reached Anuradhapura on the second day. The army had indeed taken the situation in hand. We had to dismount from the taxi and walk the last mile or so, negotiating our way past army roadblocks. Eventually we came to the honey-coloured walls of the compound leading to the shrine, and a sentry allowed us to pass.

The original fig tree under which Buddha found enlightenment in the 6th century BC grew in northern India, close to the river Ganges. In due course it died. Before that,

in the 2nd century BC, a cutting had been taken by a Sri Lankan princess who converted to Buddhism. It was this cutting of the Bo tree (or Pipul) that was planted at Anuradhapura when the princess returned home to convert her own people. The species, appropriately known to botanists as *Ficus religiosa*, is so revered by Buddhists all over the world that it is forbidden to burn any wood from it.

At first, when I passed the sentry and entered the compound, I felt a pang of disappointment. The red-tiled buildings of the shrine were neither old nor beautiful, although the prayer flags gave it the air of a carnival. An old man was reading his prayers leaning against the wall of an office. A group of pilgrims presented a pink lotus to my friend. But where was the most revered tree in the world? We climbed the steps (on the right of the photograph) and found its numerous trunks looked no more than 200 years old, though the source of these trunks was hidden in a concrete plinth. *Was* this the tree from Buddha's tree? Or was it the tree from the tree from the… But why not? Buddha had blessed the roots of the tree, as all good creatures were blessed, with the gift of perpetual renewal.

Outside in the compound we saw a young Bo tree scrambling up the honey-coloured walls. Monkeys chased each other round the trunk. And we caught our first glimpse of a tiger – a very benign Tamil tiger – couched in the shade at its roots.

Right: HIPPOCRATES'
PLANE TREE, PROPPED UP
IN A STEEL CAGE ON THE
GREEK ISLAND OF KOS

The Tree of the Great Healer

IF YOU PLAN TO VISIT GREECE to stir your heart with the sight of its antiquities, I recommend a visit to the island of Kos. When you get there, don't bother with the ruins of a temple to Asclepius, the god of healing; they are unremarkable. Go to the ruins of a tree, of the most famous tree in the world, after Buddha's Bo tree in Sri Lanka – the great plane tree of Hippocrates, the 'Father of Medicine'. You will find it battered but unbowed in an elegant square with a Turkish drinking fountain concealed under a Byzantine dome. The tree used to be supported by Hellenistic columns, askew after numerous earthquakes. Now its trunk is enclosed in a large, green, steel cage.

For centuries people have believed that this is the tree under which the great healer sat when he taught medicine to his disciples in the 5th century BC. I would like nothing more than to share their faith. This would make the tree three hundred years older than Buddha's Bo tree, a youngster of the 2nd century BC. But kill-joys will point out that the wood of the oriental plane tree, *Platanus orientalis*, rots relatively quickly. Today the main trunk is a hollow shell like an old gourd. True, there are large branches growing out of the cage from the east side of the gourd; and there is a new trunk, layered from a branch on the west side about a century ago, now forming a delightful dome of young branches. But I doubt whether the original tree, whose trunk is now a shell, is older than 600 or 700 years.

But wait, say the fans of the great healer. Suppose there was a plane tree there in Hippocrates' day? Of course, it didn't live 2500 years. But its roots did. Like Buddha, Hippocrates blessed his tree with a cycle of renewal and re-birth. The trunk, this old gourd, may be the fourth generation of the great healer's trees sprung from the roots.

Hippocrates' fans – and the excellent retsina one drinks on Kos – have convinced me. Of course they are right. Or, at any rate, no one can prove they are wrong.

Tulips Too High for the Bees

ONE COOL, SUNNY MORNING in April 2002, I watched an endless line of pilgrims queuing to pay homage to George Washington at Mount Vernon, Virginia, his family estate on the river Potomac, outside the capital to which he gave his name. Mount Vernon is the nation's principal shrine and a cheerful place. The crowds were good-humoured, and they knew they had to be patient. After an hour or two in line they would be ushered into the house, to be shown the plain little study where the Founding Father sat at his desk, the small dining-room where the domestic slaves would serve meals to him and his wife Martha, and the simple bed where they slept.

But did anyone in the crowd think of that pair of elegant tulip trees (tulip poplars, they are called in America), now over 130 feet high – the two trees that he planted in 1785 with his own hands (or the hands of his slaves) to embellish the view of the west lawn? As the queue shuffled forward under the two trees, I saw no upward glances. And strange to say (for no hero has been better documented or better displayed for the benefit of his admirers), there is nothing to tell you when you stand there that these are two of the last living memorials to the great man.

By 1783 Washington had decided to hang up his sword and retire, like the Roman hero Cincinnatus, to the life of a farmer. The British were beaten. America was free. He longed for the life of a Virginian planter with 10,000 rolling acres and 300 contented slaves. For the eight years when he had been commander-in-chief he had hardly caught a glimpse of Mount Vernon. Now he would sow tobacco and breed cattle and net fish in the Potomac and (above all) improve the house and extend the garden and plant new trees. Of course, his respite was short. Like Cincinnatus, he was needed in the capital. Who else could serve as President?

The two tulip trees remain the symbols of his brief escape from power and politics. They are both native American trees, like most of the forest trees he planted. Probably they were wild plants transplanted from the fields nearby, for that was his usual practice. I have chosen the larger and healthier one for my photograph. It is no giant, but taller, I think, than any tulip tree outside America. It is certainly a shrine – or deserves to be one. Perhaps I have stretched a point by including it among the Methuselahs. But 215 years is a long time for a tree in a garden. I should hope that both trees would live for centuries more. But I rather doubt it. Storms have already begun to gnaw at their trunks and branches; the wood soon rots, once the skin of bark is punctured.

Fortunately, a group of enthusiasts have realized the importance of the trees and arranged to propagate saplings and put them on the market. But where are the seeds? It turned out that the trees were too tall for bees to be able to pollinate the flowers. A 130-foot crane to the rescue! Watched by millions on television, a human 'bee' was hoisted by crane to the top of the trees, where he successfully hand-pollinated the flowers.

Opposite: TULIP TREE PLANTED AT MOUNT VERNON, VIRGINIA BY GEORGE WASHINGTON IN 1785

The Tree with Nine Wives

As THE ANCIENT CAPITAL of the kings and queens of Madagascar, Ambohimanga (Blue Hill) was until recently a sacred place, closed to travellers. Every wooden palace building, every sacrificial stone, every twisted fig tree had its solemn associations and its dark rituals. When a tree died, its corpse was too holy to remove, so it was left standing, a new monument to the long-dead rulers of the Merina dynasty that was abolished by the French colonial authorities in 1897.

Today's Madagascar is independent, proud and poor – and foreign tourists are welcomed to Ambohimanga. To reach the citadel, we passed through one of the famous gates: a single, enormous disc of stone to be rolled every night across the gateway.

The palace of King Andianampoinimerina (1787–1810) crowns the ridge. When your eyes become accustomed to the darkness, you see that the palace is a tall, one-roomed wooden hut, full of clay cooking pots, its roof supported by a 30-foot-long trunk of rosewood. There is one stool and two bunk beds – for the King and one of his wives. Outside, ancient fig trees shade the compound where the King dispensed justice and sacrificed to the gods.

The 250-year-old fig tree *(Ficus baronii)* in my photograph is the lower of the two sacred trees immediately below the palace. On solemn occasions, when the King presided, his 12 wives sat on 12 stone seats arranged in a circle around this lower tree. My guide, a charming schoolgirl, began counting the stones that were still visible, although half digested by the fig tree. 'Look. There's still room for nine wives.'

I wondered what grim rites those wives, and that sacred tree, had witnessed. Ambohimanga ceased to be the capital in 1810. But until the last decades of the century it was still used as a royal retreat. Queen Ranavalona had hundreds of Christian converts burnt at the stake. I wandered through the palace compound looking for relics of British influence in the years before their rivals, the French, seized power. In the summerhouse of Queen Ranavalona II I found one: a rather wretched little mahogany sideboard, presented to the Queen on behalf of Queen Victoria by the man who defended British interests in Madagascar from 1863 to 1883, my unfortunate namesake, Consul Thomas Pakenham. I am not surprised the French got Madagascar.

Right: THE CEREMONIAL FIG TREE AT THE ROYAL PALACE AT AMBOHIMANGA, MADAGASCAR. STILL ROOM FOR NINE WIVES

Bowing Politely to the Camphor Trees

Opposite: The camphor at
Atami, second biggest tree
in Japan. Each circle
round the tree, in the
correct direction, adds
a year to your life

I FLEW INTO JAPAN with an 18th-century buzzword buzzing round my head: *sharawadgi*. It means 'pleasing irregularity', I think, and it was used by Sir William Temple, the diplomat and man of letters, to describe the style of oriental gardening derived from the twisted natural forms of rocks and trees. But some people think Temple invented the word. Anyway, I had come to Japan to see the giant camphor trees, which I had heard were famous for their natural irregularities.

The biggest-girthed trees in Japan are the camphors *(Cinnamomum camphora)*, giant evergreens that grow close to the sea in the warmer parts of the country. In November and December 2001 I travelled for hundreds of miles south of Tokyo, speeding in the eerie silence of the Shinkansen (bullet train), to hunt down and photograph the camphors. I saw most of the biggest. But I found to my surprise that they don't grow in forests. They grow in the overcrowded Shinto shrines of small towns and suburbs. The trees themselves are considered sacred and are decorated with ropes and tassels or paper ornaments. Japanese tourists go by the busload to visit them, to offer a silent prayer to the spirit of the tree – or to stare in wonder. These Japanese are dressed in European clothes, but I am glad to say that they still smile and bow like their ancestors. I watched a man reading the tree's notice-board, muttering, with delight: 'Two thousand years, two thousand years.' I suppose that there are so few ancient buildings in Japan, what with wars and earthquakes and a tidal wave of new wealth, that ancient trees receive more respect than in western Europe.

Perhaps these trees really do pre-date the 7th- or 8th-century Shinto shrines where they have found a home. Personally I doubt it: camphor wood is surely not durable enough to survive more than a millennium. But, however old they are, these giants have not been allowed to grow old gracefully. Every twisted branch, every splayed trunk has been cut and mutilated to keep the trees within bounds and to protect worshippers from falling branches. Many trees have been shorn of all character. Would it be kinder sometimes to let an ancient tree die in dignity?

Twice, however, I encountered a giant with an overwhelmingly strong personality.

At Atami, a pretty seaside town 45 miles south-west of Tokyo, I saw the camphor that is Japan's second largest tree. Although the Shinto shrine is now overshadowed by two railway embankments, it is a holy place by a small ravine. I found busloads of worshippers circling the great tree in silent wonder. (Each circle, I was told, could add a year to your life. I gave myself an extra decade going anti-clockwise – only to be told that this way the magic worked in reverse. There was just time to undo the spell and restore my lifespan to normal.) Although severely mutilated after a tsunami struck the coast in the 1970s, the camphor has two huge trunks splayed like fingers, and a bole like a cliff, which dwarfs the shrine attached.

Nearby, half hidden in a young grove, was another ancient camphor, perhaps even older than the giant, but a fraction of its size. In its hollow shell a miniature shrine had been installed.

The second encounter followed two days later when I climbed the steep steps to the Shinto shrine at Takeo, 600 miles south-west of Tokyo, and was directed by a priest to the '3000-year-old' giant camphor nearby. Takeo itself didn't look very promising, owing more to California and the culture of 'Big Mac' than to the Japan we know from the woodcuts of Hokusai and Utamaro. In the suburbs there were groves of concrete poles and thickets of electricity wires. But the shrine was in a wooded knoll above the town.

The camphor was about 120 feet high and 66 feet in girth, making it the sixth largest tree in Japan. But that was not its greatest distinction. In decay it was extraordinarily beautiful. No one had smoothed out its cavities or tormented its branches and trunks with chainsaws. Unlike the other giant camphors I had seen, it had been given refuge in a freshly planted wood of cedars and blue-green bamboo safely set back from the buildings of the shrine. It was completely hollow, its age impossible to guess, as the tree rings that would have dated it had long vanished into dust.

Outside the tree was decorated with a rope and tassels to mark it as shrine in its own right. I stepped inside – cautiously. This was a ruined tower precariously balanced above two grassy terraces. The interior was used as a chapel, lit by the jagged holes where a storm had torn huge branches from the lower trunk. There was an altar and fresh offerings of rice-cakes, flowers, candles. The shafts of winter sun shone through the jagged holes like sunlight through fretted oriental windows.

Here was *sharawagi* – on a heroic scale.

I bowed and smiled politely to the spirit of the tree.

Opposite: THE CAMPHOR AT TAKEO, SOUTH-WEST JAPAN – A PRECARIOUSLY BALANCED TOWER

Homage to a Tree Like Proteus

IF YOU TAKE THE SUBURBAN TRAIN from Kagoshima, in the south-west corner of Japan, 60 miles south of Takeo, and follow the curving line of the bay, you are presented with a view quite as arresting as the famous view, in Italy, of the bay of Naples. Ahead of you, across the blue water, Mount Sakurajima, the Vesuvius of Japan, puffs a plume of steam high into the air. To the left, a long bony ridge rising to over 6000 feet, Mount Kirishima, emerges from a bleak volcanic landscape of fume-holes hissing sulphurous gas.

Below the mountain, and concealed by a forest of firs and pines, is a well-known Shinto shrine of the same name, Kirishima. I walked through the forest and up the steps one warm afternoon in late autumn to see a Japanese cedar (*Cryptomeria japonica*) described to me as one of the most respected in the region.

By comparison with ancient camphor trees of Atami and Takeo – or its fellow cedar, Jomon Sugi, the grizzled giant of Yaku Island – this tree proved a stripling. But it was an elegant stripling: about 110 feet high and 17 feet in girth. From the graceful arc of its upper branches, and it smooth regular trunk, I would guess that it was no great age, perhaps 300 years old at the most – a spirit-haunted cedar in its prime. It must be quite as big as, and far older than, any Japanese cedar in Europe or the USA for the first seeds of the species were not imported from Japan until the middle of the 19th century. My photograph is mildly mis-leading. Japan, like the West, keeps Sunday as a holiday. Most of the afternoon, the tree was hidden by worshippers, smartly dressed in Western clothes, noisily buying forecasts of their future (paper 'fortunes' sold at the shrine) and paying their respects to the spirit of the tree. I photographed it in an unusual moment of calm.

More sociable than its gigantic American and Mexican cousins of the *Taxodiaceae* – redwoods, giant sequoias, bald cypresses and Montezuma cypresses – the Japanese cedar is a most enterprising species. I particularly admire the Protean way it can change its shape and colour. Over the years it has thrown up some bizarre varieties in Japan, and many have found their way to the West. There is 'Banda-sugi', a squashed bush with needles arranged like clusters of dark green moss; 'Spiralis' (also known as 'Granny's Ringlets'), where the bright green foliage is twisted into absurd spirals; 'Vilmoriana', a hunchback that grows only 18 inches in 30 years. Best of all is 'Elegans', which can arch its back like a sea-serpent and change colour over the seasons like a chameleon. Go and see 'Elegans' when the cobwebby, bronze foliage is covered in snow. It's a sight to rejoice in – until snow breaks the back of the tree.

Opposite: THE CEDAR AT KIRISHIMA, SOUTHERN JAPAN, A SHINTO SHRINE WHERE YOU CAN BUY YOUR FORTUNE

The Other Tree under Which Buddha Sat

WHEN I FLEW BACK TO TOKYO, early in December 2001, I found the ginkgos still honey-yellow in the pavements. Autumn was late to leave Japan, and I was unprepared for the stamina of these trees. The dullest Japanese pavement glows in autumn with their exotic, long-stalked, butterfly-shaped leaves. In the parks, beside the Emperor's moated palace, there are some enormous specimens, as big as limes or beeches in Europe. Biggest, oldest and most revered are the ancient ginkgos in Buddhist shrines.

When Buddhism reached Japan from China in the 6th century AD, the Japanese imported the ginkgo, as they were taught that it was this temperate Chinese tree, not the tropical Bo tree of India and Sri Lanka, that was the species under which Buddha had found enlightenment. So the tree is sacred in Japan as well as being grown as an ornament. (Its fruit, too, is highly prized, as it is in China, both as a delicacy and a medicine.) Indeed, it was in Japan that a Western botanist first encountered the tree. It was first described by Engelbert Kaempfer in 1712, and the name we know it by is, apparently, a corruption of the Japanese word for it, *icho*, itself derived from the Chinese word meaning 'duck's foot', referring to the fan shape of the leaf.

One evening before I left Tokyo I climbed the steps to see one of the oldest ginkgos in Japan, a huge creature dominating the Buddhist temple of Zempukuji. According to the official measurements, it is about 30 feet in girth and 66 feet high, making it far bigger than any tree in Europe or the USA.

I asked an old monk if he knew the age of their tree. He pointed to the notice that claimed the tree dates from the founding of a new sect of Buddhism, Shinran-Shonin, about 1232. Oddly enough, the Zempukuji ginkgo had much the same origin as St Francis's cypress at Verucchio. For this holy man in Japan, like his Christian counterpart a few years earlier, planted his staff where he wished to see the new temple built, and 'the staff began to put forth buds and spread branches, finally growing into a stately ginkgo'.

There is no doubt that the ginkgo will survive almost anything and come up smiling. When the radioactive smoke cleared from Hiroshima, blasted by the atom bomb, a ginkgo was found 800 yards from the epicentre of the explosion. The trunk had been destroyed but the roots threw up new sprouts, and today the tree is one of the wonders of Hiroshima.

Right: THE GINKGO AT ZEMPUKUJI, TOKYO, BELIEVED TO HAVE BEEN PLANTED IN 1232

CHAPTER FOUR

DREAMS

PRISONERS

Prospero (to Ariel):

If thou more murmur'st, I will rend an oak,
And peg thee in his knotty entrails, till
Thou hast howled away twelve winters.

William Shakespeare. The Tempest

The Men They Locked into Trees

ABOUT 4 MILES OUT IN THE BUSH, half hidden when you drive along the road from Derby to Broome, is one of the most famous (or perhaps infamous) trees in Australia. It's the 'Prison Boab', a huge, brown, hollow sphere of a tree (*Adansonia gregorii*, the western Australian species of the baobab). It was once mutilated by graffiti, but a small wooden fence now mercifully protects it from admirers. This is the tree used as a prison for Aboriginal prisoners at the turn of the century. Caught by the police for stealing cattle – on land that the Aborigines considered, with some justice, to be their own – they were chained together and marched across the bush to be tried in the courthouse at Derby. On the last night of the march they were chained up inside the Prison Boab. This is the story told to most Australian tourists.

Aborigines tell it slightly differently. Their fathers or grandfathers were chained up in the *shade* of this tree, not inside. The tree had sacred associations for their people, like many of the more ancient boabs. It had been used as a mortuary, for the bones – and spirits – of their ancestors.

It's not impossible to reconcile the stories. Hollow boabs were certainly used as temporary lock-ups in certain cases – for example at Wyndham, 400 miles to the north-east. But these extraordinary trees have always been central to the life of the Aboriginal people. They are scattered in their tens of thousands over 600 miles of the Australian outback. No one knows how old they are, any more than they know the age of their cousins, the African and Madagascan baobabs. But the oldest must be well over 1000 years old. There are boab behemoths 80 feet in girth, and their vast hollow shells have protected generations of Aborigines. The same tree has served as larder, hut, hall, church – and perhaps prison.

Back in Derby, I visited a boab with happier associations, the 'Dinner Tree'. Drovers corralled the cattle here, and halted for a meal, when taking the cattle down to the harbour at King's Sound for export to Perth or beyond. I ate my ham sandwich under its shade, bewitched by the boab's fragrant, white, moth-pollinated flowers just above my head.

Preceding page: THE 'PRISON BOAB' AT DERBY.
Pages 112–13: A BOAB IN FLOWER AMONG THE
ANT-HILLS NEAR DERBY, NORTH-WEST AUSTRALIA.
Right: THE DINNER TREE AT DERBY

ALIENS

O, art thy sighing for Lebanon
In the long breeze that streams to the delicious East?
Sighing for Lebanon,
Dark cedar, for thy limbs have here increased
Upon a pastoral slope, as fair
And looking to the south, and fed
With honeyed rain, and delicate air.

Alfred Tennyson. Maud

Preceding page: CALIFORNIAN REDWOODS AT ROTORUA, NEW ZEALAND. ONLY A CENTURY OLD AND GOING LIKE ROCKETS

Right: DETAIL OF REDWOODS AT ROTORUA. THE NATIVE TREE FERNS ARE HAPPY, TOO

The Pink Beanstalks of Rotorua

MY FIRST ALIEN is a coast redwood (*Sequoia sempervirens*) incongrously sharing the five-acre park at Rotorua, New Zealand, with the local tree ferns and the black and white tui-birds. These precocious pink Californians have grown like beanstalks, doubling the speed they could manage at home. They topped 200 feet in 1980, though planted only in 1901. The authorities had some spare ground to experiment with exotic breeds of tree, and chose two species – the redwood, which they thought was a gamble, and the European larch, which they believed was a safe bet. It was the safe bet that failed, and the gamble that succeeded beyond their wildest dreams.

All the trees of the Pacific coast of America seem to be happy in North Island, New Zealand – too happy, many New Zealanders would say. The native giants, kauris and totaras, cannot compete with these pushy immigrants. Two Californian trees in particular – the Monterey pine and the Monterey cypress – have now come to dominate the windy plains of New Zealand. Ironically, it is these trees that suffer most from the wind in their native home beside the Pacific.

Still, the growth of the redwoods at Rotorua is prodigious even by New Zealand standards. A forest that has grown over 200 feet in 80 years! No exotic species, planted as a forest, has ever grown at that speed in Europe. And, of course, no native species in Europe could reach that height if you gave it a thousand years. Is there any explanation for the miracle of Rotorua? I have heard one, and you must make of it what you can. Rotorua is famous for its mineral waters and thermal baths. So the redwoods take the mineral waters like athletes taking hormones. Tell it to the tui birds.

Another poser. Will these pushy immigrants eventually overtake their ancestors in the coastal forests of California and become the tallest trees in the world? The Monterey pines and cypresses have certainly overtaken their ancestors. But their ancestors never grew very large back at home. The coast redwoods of California live on the fat of the land: deep valleys, spongy soils, a moist climate. I think it will be several hundred years before these New Zealand upstarts catch up.

A Line in Defence of the Governor

EARLY IN 1707 THE GOVERNOR of the Cape of Good Hope, Willem van der Stel, by far the most powerful white man in southern Africa, received an extremely unpleasant letter from his employers, the Dutch East India Company, who had controlled the Dutch colony at the Cape since its foundation in 1602. He was to return to Holland immediately. He was not merely sacked – he was disgraced and impeached.

Kicking and screaming, so to speak (for Van der Stel had enemies to kick and friends to scream to, but it didn't save him), he was packed off back to Holland, never to return. He left behind the largest and most beautiful of the Dutch estates at the Cape. It's called Vergelegen and is about 30 miles from Cape Town. Van der Stel grabbed half the colony and made it his private paradise. At home he lived like a prince. His garden at Vergelegen was laid out with all kinds of exotic aliens, including the 300-year-old Javanese camphor trees (*Cinnamomum camphora*) you see in the photograph here.

I photographed them late one evening in 1996. A friend obligingly stood by the pillars on which the 'slave bell' is suspended. In 1835 slavery was abolished by the British government, who had grabbed the Cape from the Dutch.

But it was not for ill-treating Africans that the Governor was sacked by his employers. It was the 'free burghers' (the Dutch and Huguenot emigrants to South Africa) who had smuggled out letters to Holland denouncing Van der Stel. He had tried to corner the market in meat and wine – the two main agricultural products after grain – by giving his own agents the official contract for them.

Van der Stel's defence was that his detractors were jealous of his success. He was the most enlightened and most efficient farmer at the Cape. His vines gave the best wine. His trees were magnificent. Go and look at the line of camphor trees at Vergelegen, and I think you will find it hard to resist the Governor's arguments.

Right: THE JAVANESE CAMPHORS AT VERGELEGEN, NEAR CAPE TOWN

St Anthony's American Bouquet

Opposite: An evergreen
magnolia from America
taking over the cloister
of the church of St
Anthony at Padua

THE GREAT CHURCH AT PADUA in northern Italy, sacred to St Anthony, is full of inspiring scuptures and tombs. But the part I find most uplifting is the cloister that encloses this princely evergreen magnolia (*Magnolia grandiflora*). I photographed it one summer evening just as the fading light was beginning to catch the lower sides of the leaves, rust-brown and felted in contrast to the shiny, dark green upper sides, and the waxy, cream-coloured flowers nearly a foot in diameter. It looks like a giant in its prime, nearly 80 feet high and perhaps 150 years old.

It is hard to believe that such a formal and courtly tree – with flowers that are larger and more sumptuous than those of any other hardy tree – belongs to the backwoods and creeks of the eastern and southern USA. In fact, a European might think it quite out of place in its native haunts, hemmed in by loblolly pines in Georgia, or slumming it among the palms and the alligators of the Florida swamps. We have known it as an aristocrat for so long. In fact it arrived from America in the early 18th century, with its reputation already made. It was the lawn tree from the great plantations, not the wild tree from the swamps. You can see it in that coastal plain today, a pyramid of shiny leaves and fragrant waxy flowers, decorating front lawns and back yards all the way from Washington to Texas – as it does from the French Riviera to Naples. Few other trees bring the whiff of the palace to suburbia.

What would St Anthony have made of this tree in his cloister? Like St Francis of Assisi, he took a delight in the wonders of nature. I think he would have loaded the altar with those waxy, white flowers.

A Fossil Aussie for Bussaco?

WHEN WELLINGTON, COMMANDER OF THE BRITISH FORCES fighting the French in the Peninsula in 1810, decided to dig in below the crest-line at Bussaco, in north-west Portugal, he naturally chose the position for its tactical strength, not its botanical interest. But the Carmelite monks, whose monastery Wellington made his HQ the night before the battle, had for years been planting exotic trees, such as the 'Cedar of Goa' (actually a Mexican cypress) on this romantic hillside. Wellington won the battle, an early victory against Napoleons's armies in a series that would end five years later at Waterloo. We don't know what Wellington thought of the trees at Bussaco – except that he tied his horse to an olive-tree, according to tradition, and the tree, much decayed, is still shown to British visitors.

Today Bussaco is best known for its park and the exotic trees planted there in the last 300 years. The monks were expelled in 1834, and the kings of Portugal grabbed it. As a royal estate, it remained a showpiece of eccentric trees. One of the dottiest is this bunya bunya (*Araucaria bidwillii*) from the subtropics of Australia, planted here in the late 19th century. The climate is so mild in this part of Portugal that frost-tender trees not only survive the winters; they grow as big as they would at home. I have seen bunya bunyas a great deal poorer in the Lamington rain forest west of Brisbane. This one at Bussaco now grows in an appropriately bizarre setting: the terrace of a palace designed for the king by one of Richard Wagner's scene-painters. On the collapse of the Portuguese monarchy, the palace was turned into a luxury hotel with stirring ceramic murals of Wellington beating the French. I ate my sandwiches admiring the bloated trunk of the tree.

The bunya bunya is one of 40 members of the monkey-puzzle family (Araucariaceae) from the southern hemisphere, trees that have dazzled (and outraged) Europe with their grotesque, spiky branches and reptilian, scaly leaves. Best known is the monkey-puzzle itself, which has made its home high in the Andes, and is therefore hardy in north-west Europe. Its three Araucaria cousins from Australia – the bunya bunya, the Norfolk Island pine, and the hoop pine – can grow only in the mildest parts of Europe, such as western Portugal.

But there is a fourth cousin in this controversial family of Araucariaceae, an Aussie teenager that is about to be launched on the world. This is the extraordinary new species *Wollemia nobilis*, alias the wollemi pine (pronounced 'wolle-my', the Aboriginal for 'look at me',) that had previously been known only from fossils. It was discovered by a park ranger called David Noble when abseiling in Wollemi National Park in the Blue Mountains near Sydney in 1994. Less than 40 adult individuals were found, mostly of the same clone, and all hidden in a botanical Shangri-La, a single, inaccessible canyon.

Wollemi offspring from the 40 survivors of this new species will soon be for sale, and it's possible they will be hardy in Britain and Ireland. I have seen one in Sydney Botanical Garden, locked in a steel cage to protect it from well-wishers. If you find monkey-puzzles repellent, you'll feel even more distaste for the wollemi. But I'll do my best to grow one. And I hope I'll be eating my sandwiches very soon under a wollemi beside the bunya bunya on the terrace at Bussaco.

Opposite: THIS BUNYA BUNYA AT BUSSACO, PORTUGAL IS ONE OF THE MONKEY-PUZZLE FAMILY FROM AUSTRALIA – AND NO MORE OUT OF PLACE THAN THE WAGNERIAN HOTEL BEHIND IT

Knees-up at Santorso

MY FINAL ALIEN IS AN AMERICAN CREATURE from the swamps, a bald cypress (*Taxodium distichum*) incongruously frisking about beside the ducks and geese on a small pond in the grounds of the Villa Rossi at Santorso, northern Italy. Wherever it's warm and wet in eastern and south-eastern America, from Virginia to the Gulf of Mexico, the bald cypress raises its elegant pale green head. ('Bald' means simply deciduous.) In the Everglades, a few hours from Miami, Florida, there are bald cypresses as tall as church spires that romp around in the mud like water buffaloes.

In north-west Europe the tree usually finds the summers too cold or too dry to make it comfortable. This bald cypress at Santorso is in its element: spring water and hot summers. Beside it grow three others nearly as large. What gives it especial distinction are the colony of pneumatophores beside its ribbed, cinnamon-barked trunk. For a long time botanists could not explain why mature bald cypresses, when they were happy, produced these strange protuberances like miniature pinnacles around their trunks. What was their point? No one could imagine. Eventually botanists realized that they must be a device for bringing air to the roots when the base of the trunk was partly or wholly submerged. (Once the tree is a fair size, it can grow in the water.) In short, a natural snorkel. The ordinary name for them is 'knees' – hardly appropriate for such a surreal appendage.

Left and opposite:
THE BALD CYPRESS FROM
AMERICA THROWING UP
'KNEES' AT SANTORSO,
NORTH ITALY – A SIGN
THAT IT'S HAPPY

LOVERS AND DANCERS

Pieria's beeches heard the measures flow
And left their mountain for the vale below.
There, listening captives of his tuneful hand
In order ranged, the green memorials stand.

APOLLONIUS RHODIUS (3RD CENTURY BC)

THE BEECH TREES COME TO HEAR ORPHEUS' MUSIC.

Kiss Me, I'm a Baobab

AFTER 1897, WHEN MADAGASCAR became a French colony and the French began to explore the botanical riches of the island, they soon made the astonishing discovery that these included six species of baobab compared to only two in the rest of the world. The six species of *Adansonia* – *za, grandidieri, rubrostipa, perrieri, suarezensis, madagascariensis* – were protean. Think of a homely shape, and you can find a Malagasy baobab to match it: a jug, a bottle, a teapot, a tumbler, a candlestick, a factory chimney.

In Part 5 of this book, Trees in Peril, you will see some of those homely shapes, but in this section I have chosen two that are rather more daring. The first of these twin-trunked trees entwined like lovers are known as 'Les Baobabs Amoureux', the Amorous Baobabs. They have been identified by experts as a romantic version of *Adansonia za*. The second pair look convincingly baobab-like, but are apparently a different genus – *Pachypodium geayi*, the elephant's foot. What an inappropriate name for these happy lovers!

The botanical puzzle remains. Why does Madagascar, largely barren, and only 800 miles by 200 miles, have three times as many species of baobab as the whole African continent and Australia combined? Palaeobotanists have produced various theories, but there is no consensus. Most theories originate from the idea of Gondwanaland, the southern super-continent that dominated the southern hemisphere roughly 100 million years ago. What are now the separate continents of South America, Africa, India and Australasia were then merely regions of Gondwanaland. And it was in these regions that evolved the ancestors of the trees and other plants we know today. When the good ship Madagascar drifted away from Africa roughly 50 million years ago – according to the theory of continental drift – it happened to carry most of the proto-baobabs on board. Only one, the ancestor of *A. digitata*, was retained in Africa. Only one other, *A. gregorii*, drifted away on board Australia.

But why are there are no baobabs native to the other continents that once made up Gondwanaland, especially in the plains of India, which have just the hot, dry climate the baobab longs to bask in? To explain this, some botanists have suggested that the Australian baobab did not arrive with the rest of Australia 50 million years ago. It floated there from Madagascar much later as seed in a nut. It sounds far-fetched, the idea of a Malagasy nut sailing halfway round the world to colonize a distant continent. But nuts do make long ocean-going journeys – and arrive still fit enough to breed. The classic example is the amazing coco-de-mer, a palm native only to the Seychelles, whose nuts have founded colonies thousands of miles off without any help from man. True, the coco-de-mer, weighing up to 40 lb, and thus the largest nut known in the world, seems well equipped for seafaring. (It's also a shape so daring that it used to make ladies blush and gentleman goggle.) But the Malagasy baobab nut may well have colonized north-west Australia. If it did, it will have joined other plucky immigrants taking this route across the Indian Ocean, including the enormous, fossilized egg of the extinct elephant bird found recently on an Australian sand-dune.

Preceding page: BAOBABS CANOODLING AT TOLIARA, MADAGASCAR – OR ARE THEY ELEPHANT'S FEET?

Opposite: 'THE AMOROUS BAOBABS' NEAR MORONDAVA, MADAGASCAR

Left: THE TANZLINDE
(DANCING LIME) AT
GRETTESTADT, BAVARIA. THE
ORCHESTRA PLAYED ON THE
FIRST FLOOR, WHILE THE
DANCERS CIRCLED BELOW

When the Band Played in the Tree

WHEN JOHN EVELYN PUBLISHED his famous book on trees, *Sylva* (1664), western Europe was full of ancient lime trees planted (or self-sown) at the centre of cities, towns and villages. Evelyn singles out some of the more famous: at Neustadt in Germany, Zurich in Switzerland and Cleves in the Low Countries. (It is the third that I believe is the tree depicted in the 17th-century engraving on page 130). All these ancient trees were ritually pruned and supported on a framework of wooden props or stone pillars.

What Evelyn doesn't say, and possibly didn't know, was that this particular form of pruning on the Continent allowed the trees to be used as *Tanzlinde*, dancing limes. This was for special occasions when the tree became the centre of festivities. The custom of decorating a tree and dancing round it must go back to the days of pagan tree-cults. In May it was honoured in many ways, especially with a maypole, a tree cut down and set up on the village green for the purpose, or with a living tree – in French, the *mai* – gorgeously decorated for the occasion. It was the *mai* in France that was taken over in the 1790s by the *sans-culottes* as the Tree of Liberty, and came to share the town centre with the guillotine.

The *Tanzlinde*, dancing limes, were more ancient and more benign. Most have now vanished, as the trees collapsed or were cut down to make room for car parks and roundabouts. But a few remain, cherished in quiet towns and villages like those of northern Bavaria. I photographed this one at Grettestadt, west of Bamberg. There's a notice saying '*1590 Stufenlinde*' (1590 'Step lime', that is, lime pruned in storeys). But the date must refer to an earlier tree, not this one. I would guess that this one's only about 150 years old, a boisterous, seven-storey youngster. The lower storeys are there for practical reasons, the upper for ornament. On May Day the youths and maidens of the town danced wildly round the trunk inside the octagon of wooden pillars. The village orchestra played all night for them, sitting on a platform above their heads in the tree. Heaven knows who was on the storey above – or what they were up to. That was the way it was in Grettestadt. Alas, poor *Tanzlinde*. Its storeys are still ritually pruned (today by the town's fire brigade). But the youths and maidens confine their dancing to the local disco.

SNAKES AND LADDERS

Of Man's first disobedience, and the fruit
Of that forbidden tree whose mortal taste
Brought death into the world and all our woe.

JOHN MILTON. PARADISE LOST

The Tree that Became a Village

IN 1829 ROBERT MOFFAT, the celebrated British missionary (whose daughter later married David Livingstone), was trekking north along a sandy track through the South African bush 1000 miles north of Cape Town. The country was half-unexplored; the Great Trek was still a few years ahead, and the Boers had yet to carve out their trekkers' republic and call it the Transvaal. A few miles west of where the town of Rustenburg stands today, Moffat's 'attention was drawn by a beautiful and gigantic tree (a species of *Ficus*) standing in a defile leading into an extensive woody ravine'. Let Moffat continue with the story as he solemnly related it in his journal.

'Seeing some individuals employed on the ground under its shade, and the conical points of what looked like houses in miniature protruding through its evergreen foliage, I proceeded thither and found that the tree was inhabited by several families of Bakones, the aborigines of the country. I ascended by the notched trunk and found, to my amazement, no less than 17 of these aerial abodes, and three others unfinished. On reaching the topmost hut, about 30 feet from ground, I entered and sat down. Its only furniture was the hay which covered the floor, a spear, a spoon, and a bowl full of locusts… I asked a woman, who sat at the door with a babe at her breast, permission to eat. This she granted me with pleasure and soon brought me more [locusts] in a powdered state. Several more females came from the neighbouring roosts, stepping from branch to branch to see the stranger, who was to them as great a curiosity as the tree was to him… They adopted this mode of architecture to escape the lions which abounded in this country.'

Moffat's story of 17 huts in a fig tree beleaguered by lions, illustrated by a picture by Thomas Baines based on a sketch made by Moffat, seemed a bit hard to swallow. But who could doubt a missionary's word? And did the fig tree exist now? Historians and botanists hunted in vain. Then one day in 1967 a South African botanist, Professor P.R.Kirby, stumbled on a huge, ancient wild fig (*Ficus ingens*, the mighty fig) on a farm called Bultfontein, close to the track that Moffat had followed. Everything seemed to him to fit: location, age, size – and there was even an African story told to the first white farmer that people remembered Moffat climbing the tree.

I went to Bultfontein myself in 1999 to track down the tree. It's certainly huge and still getting larger. Seven of the massive branches have struck new roots where they touch the ground. The tree itself covers about 120 feet with its shade. But was there really room for *17* huts on those branches? Perhaps there was. During the Boer War (1899–1902) the tree was apparently refuge for several families of German farmers hiding from both the British and Boers. At present there's only one hut – or rather the ruins of one hut.

A friend risked her life climbing the ladder. She's allergic to bees and the tree was humming with them. She found nothing in the hut – not even a spear, a spoon or a bowl of locusts. Later we found the ruined hut is a modern ruin, left over by a T.V. company filming *Robinson Crusoe*.

Preceding page: 'THE INHABITED TREE' – LITHOGRAPH BY THOMAS BAINES BASED ON ROBERT MOFFAT'S SKETCH IN SOUTH AFRICA IN 1829

Opposite: THE INHABITED TREE TODAY – ON A FARM CALLED BULTFONTEIN

Below and opposite:
CORKSCREW BEECHES
AT VERZY, NORTH-EAST
FRANCE. WERE THE
MONKS TO BLAME?

The 800 Corkscrews of Verzy

IT'S AN ALARMING EXPERIENCE to stand in the heart of the forest on the hill above Verzy, about 10 miles from Reims in north-east France. Invisible below are the vineyards with their reassuring bustle and those great names – Veuve Cliquot, and so on – that have made champagne the just reward of wealth and success. In the March sunshine the vines, still leafless, are being pruned into arabesques. Above, in the cathedral-like calm of the forest, all seems natural. And so, we are told, it is.

But wait. Why are so many of the beech trees deformed? Why are they twisted into shapes more intricate than vines, indeed twisted beyond the dreams of nurserymen – pendulous, stunted *tortillards*?

Ever since the 17th century, people have puzzled over these 'corkscrews' scattered among the beech and oak and pine. Known as *les faux de Verzy* (*fau* is an old French word for 'beech', derived from the Latin *fagus*), they are concentrated at the top of a wooded hill once famous for its holiness. St Basles, who converted the heathen in Lorraine, and St Rémi, who made Reims the spiritual centre of France, both lived here as hermits. For over a thousand years – from the 7th century – the Abbey of St Basles dominated this part of the forest. Then, at the Revolution, the abbey was sold for building stone and its ruins were lost in the grass. The mystery remained. How to explain the *tortillards*?

I went there in the early spring of 2002, expecting to find a few dozen oddities among the tall and upright beech trees in which French foresters so justifiably take pride. I found there were 800 *tortillards* at the last count. The experts say they are a genetic mutation of the common beech (*Fagus sylvatica*).

A few have spread by seed, without reverting to the ordinary form. Most of them breed by layering. The experts assure us that the *faux* are a perfectly natural phenomenon – and no one should blame St Basles and his monks. But they confess it is an 'enigma for science' why this occurred at the site of the monastic garden at Verzy, and on such an enormous scale. Elsewhere, in Germany near Hanover, and in Sweden near Malmo, the phenomenon is limited; those wild populations of corkscrews are likely to die out. At Verzy the freaks seem to be taking over.

I know I may sound alarmist, but I think someone should think of the threat to the vineyards below the hill. At the very least, we should stock up with a few more bottles of Veuve Clicquot champagne.

Where Angels Didn't Fear to Tread

I WAS THINKING OF THE LINES from the black protest song 'hey, lord, ain't you a right?', as I approached John's Island, South Carolina. This is a landscape of marshes and tidal creeks – a low, flat and rather formless place – but there are also forests of sweetgum and pines and a few magnificent live oaks (*Quercus virginiana*, the huge, moss-draped evergreen oak of the eastern and southern seaboard of the USA.) It's only half an hour's drive from Charleston, but a world away from those privileged terraces of white clapboard and Georgian brick.

Black people have been in the majority on this island for at least two centuries, first as African slaves imported to work the cotton plantations, then as impoverished farmhands and servants. I had come to see the Angel Oak, a huge, serpentine live oak pre-dating by at least a century both the planters and their slaves. The origin of the name is prosaic enough. A judge called Angel married the local heiress, so the estate passed to the Angel family. But to the black slaves and their children the tree seemed aptly named. Tree cults were part of their spiritual inheritance, and they identified the python-like branches with the spirits of murdered slaves. A black teacher from the island, described how 'the people declared that angels would appear in the form of a ghost at the oak… [After] the killings that happened around the tree during slavery time, spirits were seen by people with a 'call'… they considered the angels brought the spirits there.'

Despite its sombre history, the tree today is a delightful place – especially when the April sun shines through the new crop of small, thin, elliptical leaves. I saw no sign of any angels overhead. But I saw their secular equivalent: a bald eagle, with the imperious eye of the eagle on the American coin, quartering the heavens for rats, mice and squirrels.

Right: THE ANGEL OAK AT JOHN'S ISLAND, SOUTH CAROLINA, HAUNTED BY THE GHOSTS OF MURDERED SLAVES

Going down, not Coming up

THE SEEDS OF THE RATA are small and inoffensive-looking. Birds digest them, perched in the fork of another tree, and the seeds take root, well fertilized after passing through the birds. Now it is the rata that is perched in the fork. Its roots descend, encasing the hapless tree that has given it hospitality. Wait 200 years or more and the host has vanished inside the strangler. Murder most foul! Then, like a python relaxing after a good meal, the rata assumes the air of an ordinary tree.

Look at the photograph of this rata (*Metrosideros robusta*) at Bushy Park in North Island, New Zealand, one of the largest rata ever recorded. Would anyone guess that there is a hollow inside the massive trunk exactly matching the shape of the host tree the rata strangled? And those roots look ordinary enough – until you realize that, to encase the host, they went down from above, instead of coming up from below.

The tree is not always a strangler. You see them, scarlet-flowered in spring, scattered on the edge of forests in both North Island and South Island. They must have sown themselves there honourably enough. When I was crossing a pass over the southern Alps I collected some seed to plant in my garden in Ireland. It's possible that seeds collected at such a high altitude will produce plants hardy enough for my icy climate.

If you come to my garden (we are open to visitors) watch out for New Zealand stranglers.

Left: RATA AT BUSHY PARK, NEW ZEALAND, RELAXING AFTER STRANGLING AND EATING ITS HOST

Opposite: DETAIL OF RATA

Opposite: THE MORETON BAY FIG AT COIMBRA, PORTUGAL – A TREE WITH AN UNFORTUNATE APPETITE

Trust Me, I'm a Python

GIANT FIG TREES WELCOME YOU to the tropics, with their huge, shiny, egg-shaped leaves. But beware! Many of them, like the rata, are stranglers at heart. Their seeds are small but their purple fruit, like that of the Mediterranean fig tree, is generally delicious to birds, which deposit them in forks of unsuspecting host trees.

Some fig trees use kindlier methods to make their way in the world. The Moreton Bay fig (*Ficus macrophylla*) from eastern Australia is a real gentleman. It grows to an enormous size – specimens have been known to reach a height of 180 feet – generally starting from the ground. Sydney is full of them. One day I found a whole covey of schoolgirls sitting in the branches of the giant on the main lawn of the botanical garden. The branches were bigger than those of any beech or oak that I have ever seen in Europe. Unfortunately, the schoolgirls flew off before I could raise my camera.

Instead I photographed this Moreton Bay fig incongruously sprawling over the steps in the botanical garden at Coimbra, Portugal. This magical place, 10 miles south of Bussaco, the park where I found the bunya bunya, is full of friendly pythons. I sat among their coils without the least fear for my safety. But one word of warning. The Moreton Bay fig is perfectly safe to leave with children (as the Sydney schoolgirls proved). But it has an unfortunate appetite for stone staircases. Coimbra, beware!

Right: THE BENJAMIN'S FIG
IN THE BOTANICAL GARDEN
AT KANDY, SRI LANKA –
A 'PALAVER TREE'

Two Serpents in the Garden

THE BENJAMIN'S FIG (*Ficus benjamina*) in the botanical garden at Kandy, Sri Lanka, presents a striking contrast with the anonymous fig tree on the next page. Both are serpents in the same garden of Eden. The anonymous fig is perfectly ordinary apart from its magnificent coil of roots. The Benjamin's fig is the most famous tree in the garden. Its vast dome of drooping branches gives shade to dozens of families all through the heat of the day. It is what in Africa would serve as a 'palaver tree' – a tree where dignitaries would meet and negotiate, and holy men sit with their worry beads, and children play. (I once saw a great fig tree close to the Nile in the southern Sudan. It was still known as 'Gordon's Tree', nearly 120 years after Charles Gordon, then governor-general, had sat under its shade.)

The Benjamin's fig has lowered a number of aerial roots from its branches. These suggest that it either began life as a strangler high in a forked tree (the host now encased in its tube of roots), or that it's in its nature to be a strangler, though it was actually planted as a small tree here in the garden. I don't know which actually happened. But the Benjamin's fig looks languid and comparatively unaggressive. The same cannot be said about its energetic cousin, the Indian banyan (*F. benghalensis*). There's a celebrated example in Calcutta in the botanical garden next to the Victoria Memorial Garden. Its branches put down aerial roots at such a rate that the tree is turning into a forest. Each root, heavily buttressed, becomes a new Indian banyan in its own right. A century ago it covered 30 yards of lawn. Now it covers an area 300 yards wide. I think Queen Victoria would have approved of the tree's ambitions to found a dynasty. After all, she had 40 grandchildren herself, many of whom became kings or queens.

Left: ANONYMOUS FIG TREE
UNCOILING ITS ROOTS IN
THE BOTANICAL GARDEN
IN KANDY, SRI LANKA

GHOSTS

So I put forth my hand a little way,
And broke a branchlet from a thorn-tree tall;
And the trunk cried out: 'Why tear my limbs away?'

Then it grew dark with blood and therewithal
Cried out again: 'Why does thou rend my bones?
Breathes there no pity in thy breast at all?...

DANTE, THE DIVINE COMEDY, HELL, CIRCLE VII

(TR. DOROTHY SAYERS)

Preceding page: THE STUMP OF A DOUGLAS FIR AT QUINAULT IN WASHINGTON STATE, FELLED LONG AGO, NOW THE HOME FOR A YOUNG WESTERN HEMLOCK

Opposite: WESTERN HEMLOCKS INVADING STUMPS AT HOH VALLEY, WASHINGTON STATE

Failing David Douglas

ONE SOMBRE DAY IN DECEMBER 2001, I splashed along the freeway west of Seattle in Washington State, determined to hunt down and photograph some of the great Douglas firs on the Pacific side of the Olympic Mountains. I owed it to my hero, David Douglas.

Many would say that Douglas was the greatest of all plant-hunters. Originally, a humble gardener at Scone Castle in Scotland, he died aged 35 in Hawaii, when he fell into a bull pit and was gored to death. But in his short life, criss-crossing the unexplored interior of the north-west, he discovered or introduced a cornucopia of new trees and other plants, including the Sitka spruce, and the Douglas fir (*Pseudotsuga menziesii*) to which he gave his name.

I knew that five of the biggest Douglas firs in the world were concentrated in a single pocket of old-growth forest beside Lake Quinault. My friend Bob Van Pelt, the renowned big-tree hunter, had pointed them out to me earlier that year on the northern side of the lake.

As it turned out, I failed. The trees were still there, magnificent Douglas firs miraculously snatched back from the loggers, when other great (and no doubt greater) trees were clear felled. But, like the coast redwoods further south, Douglas firs stand aloof from photographers. The pale brown, corky trunks rise from the ferns as tall and thick as factory chimneys. But the trunks soon merge into a jungle of bright green foliage, and their heads are beyond reach of a lens.

Unable to photograph a tree, I photographed a stump (you can see it on page 153). The stump was once a Douglas fir. The loggers came (presumably before this scrap of old forest was saved). They put their mark on the tree – a notch in which they wedged a plank to support the man with the axe – and down it came. The notch still disfigures the stump and glares at you like a malevolent eye. But nothing stays empty or unused for long in a rainforest. The seeds of the western hemlock (*Tsuga heterophylla*) pepper the ground, and they can tolerate more shade than the seeds of the Douglas itself. Now a young hemlock stands astride the stump, its roots encasing the Douglas like the ligaments of an anatomical specimen. There were also vast, ghostly Oregon maples (*Acer macrophyllum*) bowed down with moss.

I had failed my hero. This and the sight of all those stumps had lowered my spirits. Perhaps it was fortunate for Douglas that he died when he did (though not the way he did). He would have been proud to see his fir and his spruce planted in their millions as the main forest trees of north-west Europe. But he would have hated to see the great Douglas firs of the ancient forests vanish under the axe.

Left and opposite: GHOSTLY
BIG-LEAVED MAPLES, WITH
COBWEBS OF YELLOW MOSS AT
HOH VALLEY, WASHINGTON
STATE. THE MOSS HELPS THE
MAPLES: FIRST IT DECAYS,
THEN FEEDS THEIR ROOTS

When Moses Followed Joshua

In 1847 a band of heavily armed Mormons led by the resourceful Brigham Young (described by a contemporary as having 'the executive force of Moses and the utter lack of conscience of Bonaparte')headed west from Missouri to found their own state outside the jurisdiction of the United States. At one point as they crossed the Salt Lake desert, studded with spiky yucca trees, their supplies ran short. Young's followers began to lose confidence. But not for long. 'There,' said the great man, pointing at the twisted arm of a yucca tree, 'is Joshua welcoming us to the promised land.'

Of course Young and the Mormons got to their land of milk and honey. They founded the state of Utah – even if they were disappointed to find, the following year, that their exodus had partially failed. (They were back in the United States, as their new territory, previously claimed by Mexico, was ceded to the USA in 1848.) But Young was used to getting his own way, often at gunpoint. Some Mormons once shot down in cold blood 120 men, women and children from Arkansas who were trying to find the trail to California; the Mormons spared the younger children. Young disclaimed responsibility. He went on to be the only US governor who made a success of polygamy, advocated with the zeal of a prophet, and died in 1877 with 23 wives at home and $2 million in the bank.

And the name stuck: the Joshua Tree. I photographed this one in Joshua Tree National Park in south-east California, not far from the live oak (see page 142). The lunar landscape and boiler-room climate are better suited to yuccas than oaks. Yucca trees, like tree ferns and palm trees, are not trees, strictly speaking, as they do not grow in annual rings of bark. But nature has made them well adapted to store water in their pithy trunks and twisted branches. They can grow up to 40 feet high, and there's a champion with a girth of 15 feet. They are said to be able to survive on about four inches of rainfall a year. I would not say they are beautiful. But I hear that when it rains in spring, if it does, their agonized expressions relax and they become, for a week or two, garlands of yellow flowers.

It hadn't rained for weeks when I photographed this fearsome specimen. Then a wild thought came to me. Joshua Tree – was this really an appropriate name? The tree 'welcomes us to the Promised Land'. Could the great man have been making a grim jest? No, I think not. Young may have been a Moses and a Napoleon, but humour was not his strong point.

The Girl Who Lay under the Banyans

Left: A sacred grove in Madagascar, formed from a single banyan tree, and once used for human sacrifice

FRIENDS RECOMMENDED two excursions outside the town of Toliara in south-western Madagascar, both to sacred ground.

The first was to the tomb of King Baba, a 19th-century ruler of a local tribe, the Makilolo. I had heard that these Makilolo kings had the novel idea of giving their children *British* royal titles. They had heard about this other royal family from British sailors who came to trade for meat and fruit. But the tomb had nothing of Windsor or Osborne – just an urn and a large, broken bell lying on a heap of stones. Near by the octopus trees (*Dideriera madagascariensis*) were pleasantly alarming. This is one of the numerous endemics (a species found in the wild nowhere else in the world) that make botanists so anxious to save the vanishing flora of Madagascar. The octopus tree greets you drunkenly waving its arms, covered in huge grey thorns, which turn green with fresh growth in the rainy season.

The second excursion was to a 'sacred grove' of banyan trees (*Ficus* spp), which friends recommended as a quiet retreat. When I arrived, half an hour before sunset, there was a strange atmosphere, as I think you will see from the photograph. The gate to the enclosure was locked. I was allowed in and asked to remove my sandals. There were concrete seats for worshippers. But who or what was it sacred to? No one could say. Presumably the grove had originated in a single strangler fig, which had multiplied itself by means of aerial roots. Many of the trees were now separate, and so decayed that they were more like bone than wood. It was a forest of skeletons – not a place to linger in once darkness fell.

Back in the hotel, I was told more about the grove. Some 200 years before, in the time of an earlier King Baba, there was a terrible drought (or perhaps it was a terrible flood) that threatened the kingdom. The local priests recommended sacrificing a young girl to appease the spirits. She was buried alive, and the banyan, where animist worshippers now pay their respects, grew from her body.

I am glad I only learnt this after returning to my hotel.

A Tomb with a View

'And now that you are lying, my dear old Carian guest,
A handful of grey ashes long, long ago at rest...'

IF YOU ARE LOOKING FOR A GOOD PLACE to lay your bones – or your ashes, like Heraclitus in the poem above – may I recommend this delightful corner of south-west Turkey now called Kekova. It was formerly the Greek olive-trading port of Tristomo ('Three Mouths'). The place is full of amenities – a medieval castle to defend you from pirates, an acropolis and theatre for Greek tragedies and a luxurious necropolis. The tombs have the best view of all: to the north, the mountains of Lycia, snow-capped in spring; to the south, a languid view of the Aegean through drifts of olive trees.

The Hellenistic tombs are inscribed with notices in Greek telling tomb-robbers to keep their distance. But that was written 2000 years ago. The tombs were broken open, the corpses robbed and discarded. The sarcophagi, meaning 'flesh-eaters', have gone hungry ever since.

The olives make a perfect match with the tombs, giving the necropolis a cheerful sense of immortality. No other tree can combine the sense of resurgent life – of sprays of silver-green foliage heavy with fruit – and happy senility. The trunks of olive trees, bowed under the weight of 600 or 700 years, become gradually perforated like a colander. Then they die or blow down, or are cut down by an invading army – only to leap up, young trees again, from their ancient roots. If only we could imitate the olive!

But the Heraclitus in the poem, who lived in Caria, further along this magical coast to the west, did find immortality. As the poem concludes:

Still are thy pleasant voices, thy nightingales awake.
For Death, he taketh all away, but them he cannot take.

If my ashes are scattered at Kekova, I hope my nightingales sing in the olive trees.

Right: ANCIENT OLIVE
TREES AT KEKOVA, TURKEY,
AND LYCIAN TOMBS

CHAPTER FIVE

TREES IN PERIL

DO THE LOGGERS ALWAYS WIN?

I think that I shall never see
A billboard lovely as a tree.
Indeed, unless the billboards fall
I'll never see a tree at all.

OGDEN NASH, THE OPEN ROAD

Ashes to Ashes

DO THE LOGGERS ALWAYS WIN? Outside North America the blunt answer seems to be yes. Inside there have been battles won and lost by both sides – loggers and conservationists.

Let's start with Australia. The species that grows tallest and throws up the finest stands of timber is the mountain ash (*Eucalyptus regnans*), which once dominated much of the landscape of Victoria and Tasmania. Enormous trees, over 350 feet high – and possibly over 400 feet high – once decorated the valleys from the Yarra range north of Melbourne to the Styx river in Tasmania. The timber made excellent cheap roof-shingles and the loggers loved it. So did the Australian taxpayers, who benefited from the sales (the timber was state-owned), and the Australian farmers who wanted the land for sheep and cattle.

A century ago you could still drive out 40 miles from Melbourne and see king-size remnants. There was the Mueller tree – named after the eccentric Baron von Mueller, the state botanist of Victoria for nearly 20 years. This was photographed in 1930 when its girth at breast height was over 70 feet. Other standing giants of this species were even larger. There was also a stump called the Bulga stump, which had been girthed at nearly 100 feet, as big as the biggest known giant sequoia in California. But the kings have gone, mainly burnt in forest fires, and there have been no successors. Today a tree with half the girth of the Mueller tree is considered a giant, and there is no tree 300 feet tall.

Why has the destruction been so thorough? Compared to other giant species, the eucalyptus grows extraordinarily fast and is relatively short-lived (a 500-year-old eucalyptus would be a Methuselah). Its oil-impregnated wood makes it extra vulnerable to forest fires, a natural hazard because of dry summers. Enter the loggers and the farmers and all the other energetic white Australians. As the area of virgin forest shrank, the hazard of fire increased. And how could kings find successors if they were themselves protected in small reserves?

In the photograph on page 167 you see a stand of 70-year-old mountain ash at Black Spur, Victoria – a remnant of forest rescued from loggers and farmers by the Melbourne Water Board. Their predecessors were killed in a fire; some have regenerated from seed, others were planted. They have already passed the 150 feet mark, and present an elegant contrast to the tree ferns.

In the photograph opposite you see a mature mountain ash, with a girth of less than 30 feet, safe in a reserve about 30 miles to the east. It's the only old tree – apart from a second veteran down the track. All its companions were felled or died in a fire. A century ago no one would have given it a glance. Now the grandchildren of those who knew the Mueller tree come to stare at this relic as though it were an animal in a zoo.

The Vanishing Totara

'IN THIS WILD WOOD [AT GWAVAS STATION] we stood in amazement before several 400- to 500-year-old *Podocarpus totara*, recognizable by the long grooves down the bark. The mightiest example had a girth of 22m and we estimated its height at getting on to 100m.'

I read this authoritative report of a 1995 tour of New Zealand in the *Yearbook of the International Dendrology Society*, and I too was amazed. A totara with a girth of 66 feet and a height of 330! A mighty example indeed! Taller than any known tree in the world except the coast redwoods. I must leap on to the next plane for New Zealand before either it blew down or somebody cut it down.

Then it dawned on me that the IDS is a learned society, but can make a fool of itself like the best of us. They wrote metres and meant feet. The mighty totara's girth and height shrank to less than a third of that dazzling score.

Four years later, in 1999, I went to see the same totara, with its fellows at Gwavas Station, near Napier in North Island, and they're not to be laughed at. This towering species of podocarp once dominated large parts of both islands. It was the tree that, with the kauri, was chosen by the Maori for their war canoes. The ribbed trunks grew exceptionally straight as well as tall, and the wood seemed almost as hard as iron. Of course, those were precisely the qualities the loggers loved. In a century and a half, the tallest, straightest and finest were conscientiously logged and turned into roofing and fencing throughout New Zealand. (As late as the 1960s, magnificent old-growth forests were being clear cut, and one colossal tree, too big for the mills to handle, was bulldozed away and burnt.) Most of the old growth forests were then turned into farmland, or re-planted with faster growing species, such as Monterey pine from California. So the lost giants will have no successors.

All this adds to the importance of trees like the totaras at Gwavas Station. The owners of the 3250 acres, Michael and Carola Hudson, are famous for their exotic garden, punctuated by huge Douglas firs and splashed with the foam of rare magnolias and rhododendrons. (The family have owned the estate since 1858, when the younger son of a Cornish family came here after seducing the coachman's daughter, and being told never to darken their door again. See my *Meetings with Remarkable Trees*.) The totaras in the wild wood come as a surprise. This is what New Zealand would have looked like when the Maori first colonized it: a jungle growth of creepers and small trees out of which the great totaras rose like towers.

Michael's wild wood was too wild for the lens of my camera. But we drove a few miles to the west, where I photographed a single, flare-trousered totara preserved in a young wood. It's no giant, just a fine specimen – one of the few left in the whole of New Zealand.

Opposite: A TOTARA NEAR NAPIER, NEW ZEALAND. ONCE GIANT TOTARAS DOMINATED THE OLD-GROWTH FORESTS OF NEW ZEALAND. NOW IT'S RARE EVEN TO SEE A FINE SPECIMEN

The Man Who Fought with Giants

IN MAY 1994 A 31-YEAR-OLD CANADIAN BUSHWACKER, Randy Stoltmann, was killed in a mountaineering accident, and Canada lost the man who had fought hardest and most effectively to rescue old-growth forests from under the noses of the loggers.

The tree in the photograph is one of tens of thousands he and his friends saved – a Sitka spruce (*Picea sitkensis*) in the Carmanah valley, Vancouver Island. It's nothing like the biggest; simply a tree that caught my eye (and my camera's) in a gash cut by a storm through a wet corner of the forest, rich in clubmoss and liquorice fern.

Sitka spruce is not generally thought beautiful in Britain. But in these virgin forests I defy you to resist its charms, the sweeping arcs of its roots, the grey bark coated with moss and lichen, the violet bole that vanishes into the mysterious canopy 200 feet above.

This corner of the forest is now Randy Stoltmann's official memorial – his memorial grove – because it was here that people discovered the world's tallest surviving Sitka spruce. Now christened the Carmanah Giant, it measures 315 feet from its moss-quilted roots to its spiky, storm-battered leading shoot. It is one of a family of giant trees that was about to be felled by a giant logging company, MacMillan Bloedel, to whom the logging rights had been leased by the government of British Columbia. In this modern giants' battle, Randy and various conservationist groups in western Canada naturally took the trees' side. As soon as the loggers' road opened up the forest, the conservationists alerted the public. There was a short, desperate campaign. The giant logging company – and the politicians who supported it – began a fighting retreat.

To save the Carmanah Giant and his neighbours meant creating a big sanctuary for them. But how big was that? First the loggers offered a mere 245 acres, then 1329. The battle continued. In 1990 the government was persuaded to set aside 8876 acres in the lower valley as the Carmanah Pacific Provincial Park. But what about the upper reaches of the same watershed on whose drainage the creeks below depended? The conservationists fought on till June 1994, when the entire Carmanah watershed of 16,630 acres was declared safe from logging.

Vancouver Island is 300 miles long and the west side is still rich in ancient forests ripe for logging. I drove along mainline logging roads from which you scuttle off like a rabbit when you see headlights approaching. Oversize logging trucks, bowling along with 100-ton loads, take the full width of the gravel. The old-growth forest is a many-layered tapestry, a mosaic of habitats. But here are the simple clearcuts – rectangles mapped in offices and hacked out with chainsaws. Soon monotonous new plantations of Douglas fir will cover them like hair growing over a wound.

By 1990 it was reckoned that the loggers had clear-felled three quarters of the ancient forests that had covered the south of Vancouver Island in 1954, ripping out the trees at a rate of 20,000 acres a year.

I hope I am wrong, but I have the feeling that Carmanah was the exception. Just for once, under inspired leadership, in a battle with giants on both sides, the good guys won.

Opposite: A CANDIAN SITKA SPRUCE IN THE RANDY STOLTMANN MEMORIAL GROVE AT CARMANAH, VANCOUVER ISLAND. THE TALLEST SITKA SPRUCE IN THE WORLD GROWS HERE – RESCUED FROM THE LOGGERS BY STOLTMANN AND THE CONSERVATIONISTS

Opposite: The Nolan Creek red cedar in Washington State, third largest in the world, was generously spared by the loggers. But they took its companions. Now it's a skeleton

Lay My Bones at Nolan Creek

In 1938 the federal government in Washington DC agreed, after a long battering from conservationists, to carve out a national park 3000 miles away on the west side of the Olympic Peninsula in Washington State. This saved from the loggers four rain-swept river valleys, rich in old-growth forests – the Bogachiel, the Hoh, the Queets and the Quinault – some of whose treasures have already featured in this book. But, as so often happened in the Pacific north-west, on both sides of the Canadian–US border, the boundaries of the new park were deliberately designed to *exclude* much of the best old-growth forests.

The Nolan Creek cedar pictured opposite grew in the heart of an ancient forest west of the park. Less than 30 years ago, the loggers were licensed by the state to clear-fell the whole area. When the chainsaws reached this western red cedar (*Thuja plicata*) and people realized that it was the third largest red cedar in the world (it's 178 feet tall with a volume of 15,300 cubic feet) even the loggers' spirits failed. Generously they agreed to preserve this single tree – worth, they said, the huge sum of $25,000.

And there it stands today. If the loggers hoped the tree would show their hearts were in the right place, they knew little about trees. Of course the giant could not survive in the fierce winds of the clearcut. First the mosses and lichens, then the tree itself, began to die. Now it is a bleached skeleton with a few living branches. There is a message there, I'm sure, that the public cannot miss. How futile it is to make this mean sort of compromise, rather than saving the whole watershed, as they did at Carmanah. Imagine trying to preserve this king of the forest, when all his kingdom lies in ruins. Soon his bones, too, will lie in Nolan Creek

TEN GREEN BOTTLES

Ten green bottles
A hanging on the wall,
And if one green bottle
Should accidentally fall
There'd be nine green bottles
A hanging on the wall... etc

<small>ANON</small>

Spirits of the Forest

I HAVE A FRIEND IN IRELAND whose father used to have the odd drink from time to time. When he died my friend made a garden, with a wall built entirely of bottles, to commemorate his long life. It was a long wall. The garden was called 'the garden of departed spirits'.

I was reminded of this one afternoon as I sailed across the bay at Ifaty, north of Toliara in south-west Madagascar, in a dugout canoe. Ahead, I was told, was a privately owned reserve for baobabs (both *Adansonia rubrostipa* and *Adansonia za*) fenced in from the goats, in a spiny forest half a mile inland from the beach. The dugout sped along like a dolphin. How right I was not to take a taxi from the hotel! The sun was cool (it was winter in the southern hemisphere) and the sea was a great deal smoother than the main road.

French botanists, working for the French colonial government in the early 20th century, rubbed their eyes when they saw what botanical treasures had survived in Madagascar. There were six species of baobab, each capable of adopting fantastic forms. As I entered the spiny forest, I rubbed my own eyes. The trees took the form of demons, skulls, bottles, teapots. Bottles were the commonest. By the time I spotted the finest family group it was already sunset. And it's quite an experience to see a family of 40-feet-high bottles, the colour of pink elephants, advancing silently towards you through the long grass. I thought of my friend's garden in Ireland. The spirits *here* had certainly not departed.

Sadly, the baobabs of Madagascar, like so much of its extraordinary flora, are in danger. The problem here in the arid south-west is not logging. The wood of the baobab is not strong enough to make timber, although the bark is used for roofing. The problem here is the classic vicious circle of developing countries – poverty, overpopulation, destruction of the environment – which will end by knocking every green bottle in Madagascar off the wall.

Preceding page: A FAMILY OF BAOBABS IN THE RESERVE AT IFATY, MADAGASCAR, ADVANCING SILENTLY TOWARDS ME AT SUNSET, THE COLOUR AND SIZE OF PINK ELEPHANTS

Above: THE LARGEST BAOBAB AT IFATY, SHAPED LIKE A TEAPOT

Opposite: A DOUBLE BAOBAB AT IFATY. STEPS IN THE TRUNKS ARE CUT BY VILLAGERS IN SEARCH OF WILD HONEY

The Elephant with Only One Foot

BOTANISTS ARE OFTEN RECKLESS when they choose the names for plants, and I think they have treated this tall, elegant creature in Madagascar most unfairly. It's called *Pachypodium geayi* and is commonly known as elephant's foot. If that's what it is, then it's the foot of a uniquely elegant elephant. In fact, it's more like a tall, thin glass bottle with a tassel of branches acting as a stopper. I hunted down this one in the same spiny forest at Ifaty, north of Toliara, on the south-west coast. I knew the species well from photographs, and it's not officially on the danger list, but this was the only place I saw one in Madagascar.

The spiny forest of the south-west is as a strange as the trees that it defends behind its barriers of thorns: elephants' feet, baobabs and others. The majority of these trees and bushes are unique to the island. (Indeed, of the island's whole flora, reckoned to exceed 10,000 species, about 80 per cent are unique to Madagascar.) Spiny rather understates their vigorous personalities. They were described by a botanist as 'spiny, wiry, succulent, or with milky poisonous sap, sometimes in combination'. I had no desire to force my passage through this forest. In fact, it would have been impossible without a flame-thrower – or a goat.

South of Toliara, the spiny forest guards the coast for a couple of hundred miles and then fades away. When a Frenchman, Count de Mondave, daringly built an outpost at Fort Dauphin in 1768, he found the *absence* of spiny forest a distinct handicap. To create a suitable stockade he imported specimens of a well-armed cactus, Mexican prickly pear, from the nearby French colony of Bourbon (later Réunion). The Mexican prickly pear spread rapidly, although it did not save the count and his friends from being massacred by the Malagasy. The French settlers were imprudently dealing in slaves. By 1900, when the island had become a French colony, the Mexican prickly pear was used as a tactical weapon by the Antandroy warriors trying to block the French advance. A French column would find itself suddenly surrounded by barricades of prickly pear thrown up on every side. The French counter-weapon was the cochineal insect, imported from Mexico. The insect fed on the cactus (producing the famous scarlet dye in the process) and destroyed the thorniest barricades.

I sat in the sun watching the local farmers burn the grass. In their struggle for subsistence, cattle farmers have reduced much of the country, especially the dry south-west, to impoverished grassland. Outside a few reserves, the tall, elegant elephant's foot seems to be doomed.

Opposite: THE AVENUE OF THE BAOBABS AT MORONDAVA, MADAGASCAR, IN THE AFTERNOON SUN. I WAS WAITNG FOR SUNSET

Sunset for the Baobabs of Morondava

THERE ARE FEW AVENUES IN THE WORLD that people drive out to see at sunset but the 'Avenue of the Baobabs' at Morondava draws admirers like moths to a flame.

In fact, it's not a planted avenue. A dusty road, half an hour's drive north of the town of Morondava on the west coast of Madagascar, passes through a large grove of baobabs, the remnants of what must once have been a forest. This is *Adansonia grandidieri*, a perfect name for the grandest of all the baobabs. (It took its name from two great French naturalists, Michel Adanson and Alfred Grandidier.) The species is unfortunately rare and endangered. A recent survey by international botanists put it on the red list because its numbers are dwindling. More people to feed means less land for baobabs. There are other scattered groves as you drive from Morondava, but no one seems to look after them. Some trees have been cut down recently; you can see shoots from the stumps. Others have been stripped of part of their bark to make roofs for huts.

The Avenue of the Baobabs is a famous attraction, so it's safe – at least for the moment. (Even here I saw one freshly cut stump, and many of the trunks had been damaged.) Perhaps there are 100 trees in this whole grove, and what a picture they make: a landscape by Salvador Dali. The trunks rise like tapering metal tubes; the branches crown the trunks like propellers.

I knew the scene well from postcards (they are in every tourist shop and hotel on the island). So I hired a local taxi to take me there, with other tourists, to photograph the sunset. Ten minutes before the theatrical moment, the sun lost interest and withdrew into a band of cloud.

I returned next day, giving myself a couple of hours to set up my camera on the axis of the avenue and prepare myself for the grand climacteric of my travels. Lorries full of farm workers and farm produce rumbled along the track, throwing up dust clouds. Down came the camera off the tripod, then back up again after each dust cloud had settled.

Six o'clock. Five past. Two more minutes? The sun's shadow began to lick the base of the 15 great trunks. The pale blue sky was splashed with pink. Was this the moment? (I had never taken a photograph at sunset before.) And then, out of the crowd of friendly tourists standing beside me across the road, came a very large Belgian lady with a very small camera. She stood like a titan in front of my lens.

I swallowed. Was it for this that I had queued in the airless corridors of 89 airports, circled the globe on 12,000 miles of dusty and dangerous roads, stayed at 62 seedy motels in 18 countries? Was it for this I had risked my neck climbing up gum trees and under razor-wire fences?

Travellers, like poets (the phrase is Richard Burton's), are an angry race. '*S'il vous plaît,*' I called in a voice like thunder, and the titan quailed. My lens opened its one eye and the baobabs at sunset were mine.

Right: SUNSET AT THE
AVENUE OF THE BAOBABS,
THE GRAND CLIMACTERIC
OF MY TRAVELS

Gazetteer of trees photographed

AFRICA

Botswana
African baobab, *Adansonia digitata*, Kalahari,
Madagascar
Banyan, *Ficus* sp., near Toliara
Baobab, *Adansonia za*, near Morondava
Baobab, *Adansonia rubrostipa*, near Toliara
Baobab, *Adansonia grandidieri*, near Morondava
Elephant's feet, *Pachypodium geayi*, Toliara
Fig, *Ficus baronii*, Ambohimanga
Morocco
Argan Thorn, *Argania spinosa*, near Agadir
Republic of South Africa
African Baobab, *Adansonia digitata*, Klaserie
Camphor, *Cinnamomum camphora*, Vergelegen
Fig, *Ficus ingens*, near Rustenburg, North West

ASIA

Japan
Camphor, *Cinnamomum camphora*, Atami, near Tokyo;
   ibid, Takeo
Ginkgo, *Ginkgo biloba*, Zempukji Temple, Tokyo
Japanese cedar, *Cryptomeria japonica*, 'Jomon Sugi' (The
   Old Cedar), Yaku Island; ibid, Kirishima,
Sri Lanka
Benjamins's fig, *Ficus benjamina*, Kandy Botanical
   Gardens
Fig, *Ficus sp.*, Kandy Botanical Gardens
Fig, *Ficus religiosa*, 'Bo tree', Anuradhapura
Turkey
Cedar of Lebanon, Ciglikara Forest, Elmali
Juniper, *Juniperus excelsa*, Ciglikara Forest, Elmali
Olive, *Olea europaea*, Kekova

EUROPE

France
Common beech, *Fagus sylvatica*, Verzy, near Reims
Common oak, *Quercus robur*, 'Le Chene Chapelle'
   (Chapel Oak), Allouville, Normandy
Germany
Large-leaved lime, *Tilia platyphyllos*, 'Tanzlinde' (The
   Dancing Lime), Grettestadt, Bavaria; ibid,
   'Wolframslinde' (the lime of Wolfram von Eschenbach),
   Ried, Bavaria
Common oak, *Quercus robur*, 'Feme-Eiche' (Justice Oak),
   Erle, near Dusseldorf, Westphalia
Greece
Plane, *Platanus orientalis*, 'Hippocrates Plane Tree', Kos
Italy
Bald cypress, *Taxodium distichum*, Santorso,
Cypress, *Cupressus sempervirens*, Verucchio, near Rimini
Larch, *Larix decidua*, Val D'ultimo (or Ultental), near
   Merano, Tirol
Magnolia, *Magnolia grandiflora*, Padua
Ireland
Beech, *Fagus sylvatica*, Tullynally, Castlepollard,
   Co. Westmeath
Portugal
Bunya bunya, *Araucaria bidwillii*, Bussaco
Moreton Bay fig, *Ficus macropyhlla*, Coimbra
Spain
Dragon tree, *Dracaena draco*, Tenerife, Canary Islands
Sweden
Common oak, *Quercus robur*, ' The Kvilleken', Kvill,
   Southern Sweden

NORTH AMERICA

Canada

Sitka spruce, *Picea sitkensis*, Carmanah valley, Vancouver Island

USA

Bristlecone pine, *Pinus longaeva*, Inyo National Park, The White Mountains, California

Coast redwood, *Sequoia sempervirens*, Jedediah Smith State Park, California; ibid, Prairie Creek State Park, California

Douglas Fir, *Pseudotsuga menziesii*, (stump only), Lake Quinault, Washington State

Giant Sequoia, *Sequoiadendron giganteum*, Sequoia National Park, California; ibid, 'The Bachelor and the Three Graces', Mariposa Grove, Yosemite National Park, California; ibid, 'General Sherman', Sequoia National Park, California; 'General Grant', King's Canyon National Park, California

Canyon live oak, *Quercus chrysolepis*, Joshua Tree National Park, California

Japanese Zelkova, *Zelkova serrata*, (bonsai), Huntingdon Gardens, California

Joshua Tree, *Yucca brevifolia*, Joshua Tree National Park, California

Live oak, *Quercus virginiana*, John's Island, South Carolina

Monterey Cypress, *Cupressus macrocarpa*, Monterey, California

Oregon Maple, *Acer macrophyllum*, Hoh Valley, Washington State

Pagoda tree, *Sophora japonica*, Edgartown, Martha's Vineyard, Massachussetts

Sitka spruce, *Picea sitkensis*, Ruby Beach, Washington State

Tulip tree/Tulip poplar, *Liriodendron tulipifera*, Mount Vernon, Virginia

Western hemlock, *Tsuga heterophylla*, Lake Quinault, Washington State

Western juniper, *Juniperus occidentalis* , Yosemite National Park, California; Huntingdon Garden, (bonsai) California

Western red cedar, *Thuja plicata*, The Quinault and Kalaloch cedars, Washington State; ibid, Nolan creek, Washington State

Mexico

Montezuma cypress, *Taxodium mucronatum*, 'El Arbol' (the tree), Tule, near Oxaca city

OCEANIA

Australia

Boab, *Adansonia gregorii*, 'The Dinner Tree' Derby; ibid, 'The Prison Boab' near Derby

Mountain ash, *Eucalyptus regnans*, Yarra Range; ibid, Black Spur, Victoria

Red tingle, *Eucalyptus jacksonii*, near Walpole, Western Australia

New Zealand

Californian redwoods, *Sequoia sempervirens*, Rotorua, North Island

Kauri, *Agathis australis*, 'Te Matua Nghere' (Father of the Forest); ibid, 'Tane Mahuta' (Lord of the Forest), Waipoua, North Island

Rata, *Metrosideros robusta*, Bushy Park, North Island

Totara, *Podocarpus totara*, Gwavas Station, near Napier, North Island

Bibliography

Magazines and periodicals
The Dendrologist
The Gardener's Chronicle
The Gardener's Magazine
The Garden (1-xx)
International Dendrology Society Yearbook (1965-2001)
International Dendrology Society Newsletter (1998-2001)
Kew (1991-2002)
The Plantsman

Websites
Lonely Planet Guides: www.lonelyplanet.com
Rough Guides: www.roughguides.com
American Forests: www.elp.gov.bc.ca/rib/sdc/trees.htm
Gymnosperm Database: www.conifers.org
National Register of Big Trees: www.davey.com/cgip-bin/texis/ vortex/bigtrees

Publications
*(All publications London printed, unless
    otherwise stated)*
Abete editions, *Gli Alberi Monumentali d'Italia*, 2 vols., Rome 1990
Altman, Nathaniel, *Sacred Trees* (Sierra Club, San Francisco 1994)
Bean, W.J. and eds., *Trees and Shrubs Hardy in the British Isles*, 4 vols and
    supp. (8th edn., 1976)
Bourdu, Robert, *Arbres Souverains* (Paris 1988)
Brooker, Ian and Keeling, David, *Eucalypts. An Illustrated Guide* (Port
    Melbourne, 1996)
Carder, Al, *Forest Giants of the World Past and Present* (Ontario 1995)
Elwes, H. and Henry, A., *The Trees of Great Britain and Ireland* (Edinburgh
    1906–13)
Evelyn, John, *Sylva or a Discourse on Forest Trees* (1st edn., 1664, Dr. A.
    Hunter's edn., 1776)
Fairfield, Jill, *Trees, A Celebration* (New York 1989)
Featherstone, Alan Watson, *Trees for Life Engagement Diaries* (Findhorn,
    Scotland 1991–2001)
Flint, Wendell D., *To Find the Biggest Tree* (Three Rivers, California 1987)

Frohlich, Hans Johan, *Wege zu Alten Baumen, Band 2, Bayern* (Frankfurt
    1990); *Band 4, Nordrhein-Westfalia* (Frankfurt 1992)
Griffiths, Mark, *Index of Garden Plants. The New R.H.S. Dictionary*
    (Portland, Oregon 1994)
Griswold, Mac, *Washington's Gardens at Mount Vernon. Landscape of the
    Inner Man* (Boston 1999)
International Tree Society, *Temperate Trees under Threat* (1996)
Johnson, Hugh, *The International Book of Trees* (1973)
Johnston, Hank, *They Felled the Redwoods* (Fish Camp, California 1996)
Levington, Anna and Parker, Edward, *Ancient Trees* (1999)
Loudon, John Claudius, *Arboretum et Fruticetum Britannicum*, 8 vols
    (2nd edn., 1844)
Mabberley, D.J., *The Plant-Book* (2nd edn., Cambridge 1997)
Menninger, E.A., *Fantastic Trees* (Reprint, Portland, Oregon 1995)
Milner, Edward, *The Tree Book* (1992)
Mitchell, Alan, *Field Guide to the Trees of Britain and Northern Europe*
    (Reprint, Collins, 1979)
Mitchell, Alan, *Trees of Britain and Northern Europe* (Reprint,
    Collins/Domino, 1989)
Muir, John, *In American Fields and Forests* (Cambridge 1909)
Muir, John, *Our National Parks* (New York 1894)
Muir, John, *The Mountains of California* (New York 1894)
Oldfield, Sara and eds., *The World List of Threatened Trees* (World
    Conservation Union, Cambridge 1998)
Palgrave, Keith, *Trees of Southern Africa* (Cape Town, 5th impn., 1991)
Palmer, E. and Pitman, N., *Trees of Southern Africa* (Cape Town 1972)
Rushton, Keith, *Conifers* (1987)
Schama, Simon, *Landscape and Memory* (1995)
Spongberg, Stephen, *A Re-Union of Trees* (1990)
Steedman, Andrew, *Wanderings and Adventures in the Interior of South
    Africa*, 2 vols (London 1835)
Stoltmann, Randy, *Hiking the Ancient Forests of British Columbia and
    Washington* (Vancouver 1996)
Van Pelt, Robert, *Champion Trees of Washington State* (Seattle 1996)
Van Pelt, Robert, *Forest Giants of the Pacific Coast* (Global Forest Society,
    Vancouver 2001)

Illustration credits

Page 1: *The Inhabited Tree*. An engraving 'M. Baynes after a drawing by
    Mr. Moffatt of Litakou'. Reproduced in the second volume of *Wanderings
    in the Interior of Southern Africa* by Andrew Steedman, London, 1835.
Page 3: *Le Dragonnier de l'Orotava*. Drawn by Marchais after a sketch by
    d'Ozonne, engraved by Bouquet. French 18th century.
Page 12: *Baobab*. Unattributed engraving.
Page 24: *Hindu Fakirs Practising their Superstitious Rites under the Banyan
    Tree*. Drawn by Picart, engraved by Bell.
Page 40: A painting of the Californian big tree in the Sierra Nevada based on
    early photographs.
Page 54: *The Dwarf and the Giant*. Unattributed early 18th-century engraving.
Page 66: *Punishment of the Tcha*. Drawn by W. Alexander and engraved by
    J. Hall. London 1796.
Page 72: *The Spirits Blasted Tree*. Engraved J. Cuitt 1817.
Page 86: *The Dracaena Draco or the Celebrated Dragon Tree at Orotava in the
    Island of Tenerife*. Drawn 'on the spot' by J.Williams 1819.
Page 88: *A Hindu Family of the Banian Caste*. Drawn by J. Forbes,
    engraved by J. Bombay, 1769
Page 114: *Shepherd in the Stone Room at Newgate*. Unattributed early
    18th-century engraving

Page 118: *A Mythical Beast*. Unattributed mid 17th-century engraving.
Page 130: *'De Cleefste Lindeboom'* A Dancing Lime. Unattributed 17th century
    engraving.
Page 136: *Adam and Eve*. Unattributed 18th-century etching and engraving com-
    bined.
Page 137: see also page 1.
Page 152: *Port Famine*. Drawn by Goupil, lithograph by Emile Lasalle/ Thierry
    Freres, from *Atlas Pittoresque*, Paris, 19th century.
Page 166: *Gum forest*. Drawn and engraved by 'RE'. 19th-century lithograph.
Page 176: *Encampment under a Baobab Tree*. Unattributed 19th-century engraving.

Front jacket: The author with a grizzly giant, a Giant Sequoia in Yosemite National
    Park, California.
Front flap: The author with Giant Sequoias, Sequoia National Park, California
Front endpaper: Baobabs at Khubu Island, Botswana.
Back endpaper: The smaller of the two ancient camphor trees at Atami in Japan.
Back flap: The author prepares to climb the 207-foot Gloucester tree, Western
    Australia
Back jacket: The Avenue of the Baobabs, Morondava, Madagascar

Index

Text and photographs copyright
© 2002 Thomas Pakenham
First published as a Norton paperback 2003

For information about permission to reproduce
selections from this book, write to Permissions,
W.W. Norton & Company, Inc., 500 Fifth Avenue,
New York, NY 10110

The text of this book is composed in Sabon MT
with display set in Village Roman Titling

Design Director: David Rowley
Designer: Nigel Soper
Text Editor: Patricia Burgess
Additional Picture Research: Melanie Watson

Library of Congress Cataloging-in-Publication Data
Pakenham, Thomas, 1933–
    Remarkable trees of the world /
Thomas Pakenham.–1st American ed.
p. cm.
Includes bibliographical references (p) and index.
ISBN 0-393-04911-6
1. Trees. 2. Trees–Pictorial works. I. Title.
SD383 .P367 2002
582.16–dc21

2002021934

ISBN 978-0-393-32529-4 pbk.
W. W. Norton & Company, Inc., 500 Fifth Avenue,
New York, N.Y. 10110
www.wwnorton.com

W. W. Norton & Company Ltd., Castle House,
75/76 Wells Street, London W1T 3QT

4 5 6 7 8 9